GROWING UP CHILDREN:
How To Get 5-12 Year Olds To Behave & Do As They're Told

By

DR DARRYL CROSS

Testimonials

"Good, solid, practical advice that is easy to understand and activities that anyone can implement successfully. Our only regret is that we didn't have this available years ago!"
Carl Clappison, Chartered Accountant, Kitchener, Ontario, Canada

"In the short time that we have implemented Darryl's program, we have witnessed some amazing changes in our kids. After a couple of days, the routine is running like clockwork and everyone is happy – the previous tension has lifted.

Thank you so much for your simple and practical processes. They have had a massive impact on our life."
Jason Croston, Partner, Skaines Reeves & Jones, Brisbane, Queensland, Australia

"Being second-time-around parents, having raised our biological children and now finding ourselves with two wonderful adopted daughters in their toddler years, I marvel at the question – how did our first two survive the growing up of their parents?

Darryl's communicative style will have first-time parents finding comfort and direction as they try out their untested parenting skills, and not-so-new parents nodding their head in agreement as they relate from past experiences.

The Bible says train up a child in the way they should go, and when they grow old they will not depart from it.

Thank you, Darryl, for supporting parents in such a critical life function, raising our children. We so often must learn by trial and error."
Richard B Kendall, Principal, Gordon, Hughes & Banks, Golden, Colorado, USA

Testimonials

"Darryl has provided parents and caregivers with practical information ....

The book is easy to read, and easily shared in its e-format. Summaries at the end of each chapter enable key points to be discussed and revisited.

Adults who want guidance will find the book can be applied to different parenting situations, and most importantly, will be assisted to feel more confident in making positive parenting decisions."

Gloria Hinks, former Principal, Adelaide East Primary School, South Australia, Australia

"From a lay-person's point of view, we think this book is excellent.

It goes straight to the core of the main issues of child rearing. It asks all the right questions and then proceeds to answer them in a complete and practical manner.

We love the way that Darryl is unequivocal in his solutions. He tells parents what is wrong, not just what is right (so refreshing in these politically correct times). No euphemisms, no room for interpretation – just plain advice in plain language.

We found this to be the tone throughout the book and this is what we think sets it apart from other "how to" and "self-help" books.

Marina & Steve Whitham, Whitham Media, Norwood, South Australia, Australia

"As the father of five young children, I found "Growing up Children" to be a thoughtful and practical guide for raising kids in today's busy world...

Dr Cross' revealing insights into how the parent-child relationship can get off track, and the helpful examples for how these concepts can be applied, will enable parents to create the environment their children need to grow into well-adjusted adults.

"Parents who are willing to take the time to learn how to apply the concepts found in "Growing up Children" will undoubtedly become better at parenting, and ultimately improve their relationship with their children."

Paul Kessler, Managing Director, The Syncretics Group, Inc., Branford, Connecticut USA and Co-author of "Leading at the Edge: Leadership Lessons from Extraordinary Saga of Shackleton's Antarctic Expedition"

"I found this to be a practical, no nonsense guide for parents with primary-aged children. A highly recommended must read book that will quickly become well worn."

Leonie Trimper, President, Australian Primary Principals Association, Hindmarsh, South Australia, Australia

"This easy-to-read book is both honest and practical, taking a common sense approach to ensure children get stability and security in a constantly changing world.
Practical, positive and empowering, this e-book leaves the reader with a real sense of strength and personal control in their parenting."

Richard Wundke, Educational Consultant, Shanghai, China

"It's been a while since I've read a parenting book packed with such sensible and practical guidance.

I found this unique comparison between the wheels of a bike and balance that we as parents must have between love and rules very helpful. We must keep both wheels rolling, pumped and in good order to have balanced and loved children.

This book is a good and easy read, I really enjoyed it."

Vanessa Wrogemann, Bookkeeper, Highgate, South Australia, Australia

Testimonials

"There is a pathway to sanity!! The 'Parenting Plan' by Dr Cross has changed all our lives. The way forward now looks promising".
Jan Hanlon, Athelstone, South Australia, Australia

"I commend Dr Cross for writing this book. He gives everyday examples that I could easily understand and so very much relate to. I believe by reading this book that it has empowered me with the tools and strategies that I now feel I can easily put into place within my own family. Thank you."
Tracy Munday, Office Administrator, North Adelaide, South Australia, Australia

"Your simple methods and ideas have helped me to become a better parent and how to work with my children and not against them.
Understanding the very importance of the habits and discipline we instill in them now will create for well balanced and respectful young adults. Thank you."
Michelle Walford, Gawler, South Australia, Australia

"I think the book is excellent...I am very impressed by what I have read.... and congratulate you for offering this to parents and filling the void on bookshelves."
Sarah Hopwood, Director, and Coach for "Equipping Young Adults for Life" West Sussex, England

Other books by the same author:
"Teenager Trouble-shooting: How to Stop Your Adolescent Driving You Crazy"

Published by Booksurge Publishing
Cover design by Ian Smedman

Copyright © 2008 by Darryl Cross. All rights reserved

Reproduction and distribution in any way, shape, or form is forbidden. No part of this book shall be reproduced, stored in a retrieval system, or transmitted by any other means, electronic, mechanical, photocopying, recording, or otherwise, without prior written permission from the author.

Disclaimer

This publication is designed to provide accurate and authoritative information with regard to the subject matter covered. It is sold with the understanding that the author is not engaged in rendering legal, accounting or financial advice of any kind. If legal advice or other professional assistance is required, the services of a competent professional in the appropriate area should be sought.

The author denies any liability for incidental or consequential damages resulting from the use of the above information in this book. This book is designed to assist with generating and exploring various child-rearing options. It does not make decisions for the individual, but provides a range of options to be considered. No responsibility is accepted for any liabilities resulting for the actions of any parties involved.

ISBN: 1-4196-8550-3
ISBN-13: 978-1-4196-8550-7

Visit www.booksurge.com for additional copies

FOREWORD

"Growing up Children" is a very practical book for parents written in a lively and engaging manner by a parent and clinical psychologist. We all want the very best for our children and this book taps into that heartfelt need.

Darryl's book focuses on the formative 5–12 year old range. There are no training manuals, short-cuts or "immediate harvests" for our children. Simply and step by step, Darryl leads us through the maze of parenting a young child during these formative years.

The book is lavishly illustrated with examples from his clinical practice, which bring a very practical and realistic feel to the book. His book leads us gently through the changing landscape of parenting, provides us with guideposts on our journey and draws his expertise together in a very realistic and easily implemented program. His supplementary "hints" for parenting is a unique feature of the book. Darryl's well-grounded parenting advice provides us with very practical alternatives for parenting in more effective ways than we were perhaps parented ourselves.

It is a book that belongs in the home of every parent.

Professor Phillip Slee
School of Education
Flinders University of South Australia
Bedford Park, South Australia
Australia

CONTENTS

	Page
FOREWORD	vii
CHAPTER 1: THE CHALLENGE AND THE REWARD	1
Everyone's an Expert	1
Parenting is Hard Work	2
Where Do We Learn This Parenting Thing?	4
"Like Father like Son?"	6
Then There's the Mix	6
The Rules have Changed	7
Thou Shalt not Smack or Spank	8
Your Child has "Rights"	9
No Training Courses	11
No Training Manuals	13
No Short-Cuts & No Immediate Harvest	14
Summary	17
CHAPTER 2: THE TWO WHEELS OF PARENTING	19
Start Out With the End in Mind	19
What Do You Really Want for Your Children?	19
The Power of Modeling	22
The Two Wheels	25
How Problems Arise with Children	27
1. Wobbly Love, and No Rules Wheel	27
2. Bumpy Rules Wheel, and No Love Wheel	30
3. No Love Wheel, and No Rules Wheel	34
Unconditional Love and Appropriate Rules	37
Summary	40
CHAPTER 3: THE LOVE WHEEL	43
Love being Unconditional	43
Actioning Love	45
1. What is Over, is Over	45
2. Forgiveness is the Fragrance	46
3. Think Positively about Your Child	48
4. Listen Really, Really listen	48
5. Having Fun and Giving Special Treats	53
6. Spending Time with Your Children	54
Summary	56

CONTENTS Continued

	Page
CHAPTER 4: THE RULES WHEEL	59
Step 1: Set the Rules	60
Step 2: Set the Right Rules	61
1. The Morning Routine	63
2. The Evening Routine	64
3. Children Fighting or Not Getting On	66
4. Children Not Doing as They are Told	67
Step 3: Set the Rules Clearly	69
1. Make the Rules Very Specific with No Loopholes	69
2. Make the Rules Positively Worded	70
3. Put the Rules on a Poster	70
Examples of Rules	71
Morning Routine	71
Evening Routine	75
Children Fighting & Not Getting On	77
Children Doing as They Are Told	79
Summary	82
CHAPTER 5: MAKING IT ALL WORK	85
Setting up the Program	86
Family Conference	86
The Ingredients	87
The Program Begins	88
Step 1: Immediately Give Out Consequences	88
Step 2: Reward for Following the Rules	91
Step 3: Negative Consequences for Not Following the Rules	99
Review Time	111
Conclusion	111
Summary	113
CHAPTER 6: ADDITIONAL 17 HINTS	117
Summary	135
CHAPTER 7: FREQUENTLY ASKED QUESTIONS	137
Summary	175

CONTENTS Continued

	Page
CHAPTER 8: FREQUENTLY ASKED QUESTIONS ABOUT CHILD DEVELOPMENT AND SCHOOL	179
Summary	211
CHAPTER 9: EPILOGUE	215
ABOUT THE AUTHOR	217

CHAPTER 1

THE CHALLENGE AND THE REWARD

Everyone's an Expert

Have you noticed how everyone seems to be an expert when it comes to child raising? It's true, isn't it? Whether it is your own parents, aunties, uncles, family friends or even the next door neighbor, everyone seems to have the "truth" about what makes a good parent or how children should be raised.

Same is true, by the way, for how to be married or have a permanent partner. Everyone's got good advice. With children though, everyone has an opinion -- which reminds me of the saying I read once, "Opinions are like belly-buttons, everyone has them!"

It doesn't matter who it is, family, friends, work colleagues, even strangers – everyone seems to have a monopoly on the truth. When it comes to knowing the right way to raise children or the right way to deal with a particular situation or problem involving children, everyone seems to be an expert.

It can be difficult, especially for new parents, to work out what is good advice and what isn't. **Sometimes the "babble" gets overwhelming.**

> "He who has no children brings them up well."
>
> (Proverb)

Parenting is Hard Work

Being a parent can be downright difficult. It can bring men who are strong and dominating in their sports, their businesses or workplaces to their knees. It can bring women who are bright, capable, well-organized and outgoing to be miserable and downcast. Parenting is certainly a challenge.

I have heard many stories in which a couple was so keen to have a child that they could love, care for and enjoy. Then along comes gorgeous little Michelle or Michael. This was the baby that they wanted. This was the baby that they longed for.

> "There's only one pretty child in the world, and every mother has it."
>
> (Proverb)

However, in some cases, their dreams start falling apart. Gone is the peace and harmony, the family routine, structure and organization.

Instead, there can be stress and tension, constant disharmony and fighting. The child and the parents are out of control. This is the baby that at times the parents would gladly give away. The dream has turned into a nightmare.

The jewel in the crown has turned into the stone in the ground!

> Adrian and Louise phoned my consulting rooms to make an urgent appointment saying that they were "at their wits end" and needed to see someone straight away. They explained to my secretary that they had all but given up hope in managing their 7-year-old daughter Katrina, but had heard of me through some friends and felt they had to do something immediately. Katrina was their only daughter, and she was currently in her third year at a local school.
>
> Katrina walked into my office with her parents and promptly sat in one of the three chairs available telling her parents where they, in turn, could sit. So that we could all hear the same "story," I asked the family to tell me what had been going on. Her mother started by saying that Katrina would not do as she was told, was stubborn and strong-willed, and that they were having continual major blow-ups in the family with a lot of shouting and yelling.
>
> Father, on the other hand, seemed somewhat bewildered and powerless. He said that the blow-ups were occurring mainly between his wife and daughter. He couldn't understand why his wife would get into an argument with the daughter in the first place. Needless to say, it was causing a real rift between the parents, who argued about how to manage Katrina.
>
> I turned to Katrina and, based on what I'd heard and a hunch I had, I quietly asked her who "ran" this family. She was sitting very upright and composed in her chair with her legs straight out in front of her because she couldn't touch the ground, when she quite confidently announced that **she** ran the family. Her mother rolled her eyes and her father just nodded.
>
> Interestingly, after I had outlined a parenting program that the parents could follow and they returned for a further

consultation three weeks later, I again called all the family into my office. Katrina promptly announced that she had not wanted to come to visit me that day because she had liked the way the family was running before her first visit to see me!!

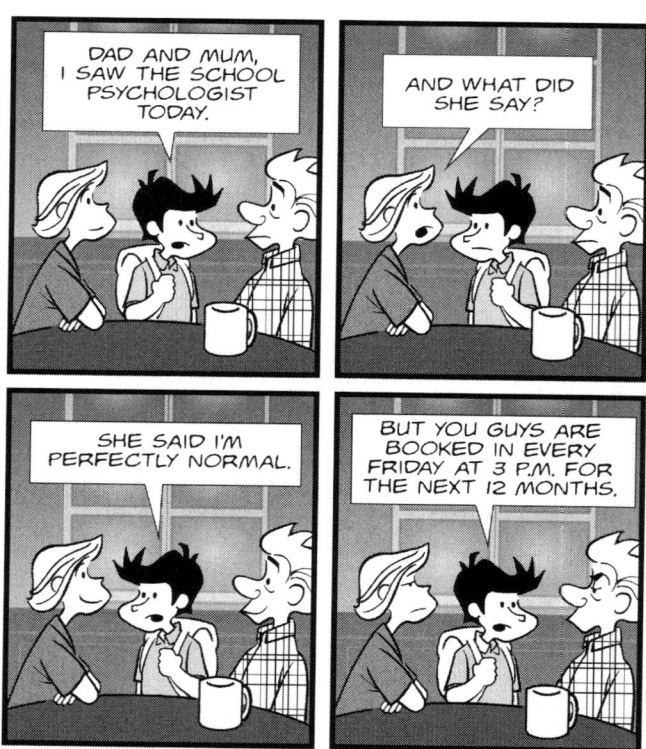

Where Do We Learn This Parenting Thing?

Let me ask you a question. Where did you learn to be a parent? I have asked that question countless times in various seminars and workshops, and always the answer is the same: *from our own parents*.

Who says though, that their parents were the perfect parents or that their parents had it altogether? What if their parents were not particularly effective? What if their parents were in fact, dysfunctional in their parenting?

What if, for example, their parents had been strict disciplinarians who believed that they should not "spare the rod" nor "spoil the child."

What if their parents were rather laid-back and laissez-faire, where they had the run of the home to themselves and there were no limits or boundaries? What if their family was full of chaos during their upbringing?

What if their family had its share of violence and aggression? What if.......?

While we talk about parents here, the same is true for a single parent. Where did he or she learn to be a parent? Where did they get their tips for raising children?

What chance do I have of being an effective parent if my only real guide for parenting is that which I received through my own parents?

Answer: Little or no real chance.

It is certainly true that the way we act as parents is modeled basically on the way that we were raised. If, by good fortune, we were fortunate enough to have received effective parenting, then our own parenting style will be similarly effective. But for many of us, it's a long shot. In other words, if we did not have generally effective parents, we will continue to struggle as parents ourselves and find it tough going.

"Like Father like Son?"

Many of us decide, however, that because we were raised in a particular way, we will **not** follow suit with our own children.

For example, there is the parent who says to me, "My father was a strict old goat who always yelled and screamed at us and I'm certainly not going to be like that with my kids."

Sometimes such parents are correct – they are not like that with their children. However, for some, the decision to do it differently means they swing to the other end of the continuum and are "soft," with no boundaries or limits on the child.

For others, although they declare that they will not follow in their father's footsteps, for example, the modeling is too great, and to their horror they find themselves doing exactly that which they didn't want to do and see themselves yelling and abusing just "like the ol' man did."

> "Having children makes you no more a parent than having a piano makes you a pianist."
>
> (Michael Levine)

Then There's the Mix

What complicates the issue even more are the **different set of parenting principles** our partner brings to the relationship based on what he or she received as they were growing up.

By "partner" I mean a husband or wife, which includes the step-parents who are in a marital relationship with the child's mother or father. It could also include the child's other parent living in the same household, which is sometimes referred to as a de-facto relationship, or perhaps another parent not living in the household.

Consequently, we have possibly two ineffective styles of parenting coming together to produce a further, yet equally ineffective parenting style!

For example, we might have one parent who is rather strict and who frequently says "no" to the child's requests while on the other hand, we have a parent who is more "soft" and who usually says "yes." Where does that leave the child? Right in the middle.

The smart children will usually exploit such differences by playing off one parent against the other. The parenting confusion continues. In fact, it's kind of amazing that any of us make it through, but such is the resilience of human life (and such is God's grace) that indeed we do.

> "My father was frightened of his mother. I was frightened of my father and I'm damned well going to make sure that my children are frightened of me."
>
> (George V; 1865-1936, King of England)

The Rules have Changed

Just eavesdropping on any conversation between parents or conversations between grandparents for example, and you'll certainly hear someone say, "It's all changed since my day."

Indeed, they would be right. It has all changed. And that makes the job of parenting even more difficult.

Not only are we struggling to cope based on our own parenting, then trying to juggle that with a partner's different parenting style, but to top it all off, someone changed all the rules.

Thou Shalt not Smack or Spank

In many places for example, the government has enforced the notion that "thou shalt not smack or spank." While I have certainly heard it said that the occasional smack on the bottom didn't hurt anyone, what the governments and bureaucrats of the day are trying to do is prevent excessive smacking and physical punishment that, as we all well know, sometimes ends up on the front page of the morning newspaper as severe child abuse and assault. So, to try to counteract the growing trend of more children being abused and assaulted, government guidelines have proclaimed that smacking or spanking is "out."

While the intent of such legislation can be readily appreciated, what the government of the day has actually done is to "throw out the baby with the bathwater." In other words, in order to try to restrain the few aggressive and violent parents in our community, the government has put a blanket ruling across everyone.

While parents were told in no uncertain terms that they ought no longer spank their children, they were **not** told what else they could do instead. If parenting was hard before, it was now darn nigh impossible.

> **We have thrown out the baby with the bathwater.**
>
> **We have been told "Thou shalt not smack," but we have NOT been told what we can do instead.**

How were they now supposed to discipline their children?

How were they going to get their children to do as they were told? What were they supposed to do to get their children to comply?

If, for example, their child was throwing a temper tantrum in the local shopping centre and the parent gave the child a smack on the legs, would they be reported to the government authorities and have the child taken away from them? (This is certainly what many parents believe.) What if the child was acting up big time in a public place and the parents spanked the child? Would officialdom be knocking on their door asking questions?

Needless to say, many parents became confused, distressed and scared.

Now it needs to be said quite clearly that I'm not an advocate of hitting or spanking children. As this book shows, there is a better way.

However, it was true that government intervention (along with other changes in our world) caused parents to lose their way. It was like, without warning, someone had turned off all the lights and left parents to flounder in the dark.

Your Child has "Rights"

Within the education and welfare sector too, there has been some social engineering and political correctness that has been introduced into the school curriculum with the notion that children have "rights." Usually this notion is introduced into secondary schooling or high school for adolescents, but somehow or other, it filters down into the primary or elementary school.

Of course, everyone has rights. However, some educators, out of their own personal or political agendas, have reacted against adult authority or people being in charge and introduced the notion of children's rights into the curriculum. Children are now clearly taught that they have rights.

Naturally enough, the school curriculum flows over into the home environment. What does a parent do (who might be loving and well-intentioned and who, for all intents and purposes is doing a relatively good job at parenting), when suddenly confronted with a 7 or 8-year-old who indignantly states that he or she will not turn off the television or will not clean up their room because they have "rights" (e.g. "I have my rights and I don't have to do it")?

Now, this is not to suggest that the school has actually said this, but it is certainly true that this is how the message is perceived by students and certainly how it's relayed to the parents at home. The parent's blood is either going to boil and the child is indeed in danger of being "abused" or the blood turns to water and the parent dissolves into a quivering mess!

> *"Parents are the bones on which children sharpen their teeth."*
>
> (Peter Ustinov; 1921-2000, British actor)

Stop Press! The headline from the Adelaide internet news site reads, *"Grounded Girl, 12, Takes Father to Court"* (http://www.news.com.au/adelaidenow/story/0,22606,23887815-912,00.html).

The story reads:
"A Canadian court has lifted a 12-year-old girl's grounding, overturning her father's punishment for disobeying his orders to stay off the internet. The girl has taken her father to Quebec Superior Court after he refused to allow her to go on a school trip for chatting on websites he tried to block, and then posting 'inappropriate' pictures of herself on-line using a friend's computer. The father's lawyer Kim Beaudin said that disciplinary measures were for the girl's 'own protection' and is appealing the ruling. 'She's a child', Ms Beaudin said. 'At her age, children test their limits and it's up to their parents to set boundaries.' 'I started an appeal of the decision today to re-

establish parental authority, and to ensure that this case doesn't set a precedent,' she said. 'Otherwise, parents are going to be walking on egg shells from now on,' Ms Beaudin said."

Is it any wonder therefore, that parents have been left floundering on the high seas of parenting with no lighthouse or beacons to guide them, and no rescue in sight should they need help or assistance?

The captains that went before them in the form of their own parents, grandparents and family are also of little help because the vessels are all different and the seascape has changed.

Parents are generally lost, but rowing hard and hoping against hope that somehow it will be alright and that it will all work out in the end.

No Training Courses

It seems incredible to me, irrespective of what has been discussed above, that there really is a complete lack of training in our community on how to be parents.

It seems unbelievable that the two most basic and important roles that sustain and underpin our whole community, that of being married or a permanent partner, and that of being a parent, involve **no** real training or instruction at all.

"Being an effective partner and parent are two important roles that underpin the fabric of our society – so how is it than we don't receive any training in either?"

(Darryl Cross)

Certainly, there are some organizations, particularly those that are church related, that do offer pre-marriage courses and that do offer short parenting courses. But generally speaking, while these are well-intentioned, they are only short courses and cannot be expected to bring about effective change in people's attitudes and behavior.

Typically too, the people who attend these kinds of courses are usually the "converted" who are probably reasonably effective in their communication and interactions anyway, and in their general ability to be parents. It's the same old story. Those who really do need such courses generally do not access them.

"How is it that almost all of us have had more training in learning to drive a car than we have had in learning to be a parent?"

(Darryl Cross)

It is interesting to ask this question: If the continuance of our society depends on appropriate parenting and rearing of our children, how come we're leaving it to chance?

Where are the intensive courses which will allow us to feel confident in our role of parenting? What are we doing to counteract a dilemma that is permeating the community – namely, parents who don't know how to be parents and yet have nowhere to turn to learn the necessary skills?

If you answered that there are government agencies available, then you would be right, but a closer look would tell you that these are understaffed and under-resourced. If you answered that there are welfare and church organizations available, then you would be right, but a closer look would also tell you that these are hopelessly under-financed.

No Training Manuals

Recently, when I bought a new washing machine, there was a comprehensive manual that told me everything I needed to know about the appliance. It even had a section at the rear of the booklet titled "troubleshooting" which has been invaluable on a few occasions.

In fact, I just purchased another digital camera and needless to say, it has come with a very well illustrated "Owner's Manual" with photos and diagrams and a clear explanation. There are particular sections devoted to specific problems that the user could encounter over time.

When each of my three children was born however, there was no such training manual and no guidelines.

The tragedy is that you and I have had more training in how to drive a car, work a computer, use a piece of software or use a mobile phone than we have had in being a parent.

I remember vividly when I first walked down the hospital steps with our first born in a bassinet and placed him in the back seat of the car to take him home. I remember feeling overcome with a general sensation "what do we do now?" There was no comprehensive booklet. There was no nurse, teacher, trainer, coach or mentor. There was no-one. Just us and this baby. And the baby was so little and so, so dependent on us. This was not exactly how I had imagined it.

"Never have children, only grandchildren."

(Gore Vidal; 1925-, USA novelist)

While this book you are reading is not strictly a manual, it is indeed a recipe book of ideas and techniques that you might find valuable.

Needless to say, the recipes are tried-and-true over three decades of working as a psychologist, of having worked in a clinical hospital setting, as well as in my own private psychology practice. I sincerely trust that this e-book will give you the tools to be more effective parents and give you greater confidence in your parenting.

No Short-Cuts & No Immediate Harvest

Some parents may see this as bad news, but it needs to be said — there are no short-cuts!

Some parents must believe that children grow up through osmosis because they do not give time and attention to their children. It may seem like stating the obvious to say that children need care and attention. In a clinical psychology practice though, I got to see scores of parents who believe that without time and attention, effort and input, their children will miraculously grow up into mature, responsible adults. They are then somewhat amazed and generally annoyed when, in adolescence for example, it all starts to come horribly unstuck.

There is no fast track. No quick recipes. No microwaving to produce the result.

Instead, it is a long slow bake.

If you are not in for the long haul, then don't put your hand up for producing babies and being a parent in the first place.

There is no quick microwaving to produce the desired result. Instead, it is a long, slow bake.

The Challenge and the Reward

It is a commitment that means once you put your hand to the plough, there is no turning back. Without wanting to be trite, the farmer does not wander out into the field at harvest time hoping that somehow, the crop will have grown and be ready for harvesting without having tended the crop. No way.

It is also important to understand that there is no immediate harvest. There are countless hours, days and weeks of toiling the soil, seeding and fertilizing, cultivating for weeds and constant overseeing before finally, the grains have matured and the harvest begins. Everyone knows this; it is a law of nature. In the same way, there are basic laws of human nature and when it comes to parenting, you have to put in the toil and time in order to reap the harvest.

And the harvest takes time. You can't speed it up. You can't make it go any faster than the laws of human development will allow.

In this fast paced world and in this so-called throw away society, which is intent on producing results and getting an outcome now and quickly, parenting is quite the opposite. The smart, thinking parent will not try to force the laws of human development; rather they will slow it down to try to enjoy the journey.

Interestingly, with this whole parenting thing, there really is no arrival or end-point because it just keeps on continuing. Of course, parenting varies at different stages in the child's life as he or she moves through the primary years into adolescence and adulthood, but the parent is still a parent.

The real product of the parenting relies very much on the parent slowing down to enjoy the journey and making the most of each stage as it unfolds and develops. It is all about enjoying the process rather than waiting for the outcome. **It is about enjoying the now rather than trying to anticipate the future**.

There is an analogy in nature that probably serves to reinforce this point. The **pine tree** for example, grows quickly and comes to maturity at about five years, at which time it can be cut down, harvested and then made into softwood or white furniture. This kind of furniture is reasonably affordable, but it depreciates quickly, loses its value rapidly and typically, does not last long.

On the other hand, the **cedar tree** grows slowly and surely over a few decades before it is ready to be harvested, at which time it is crafted into cedar furniture. The wood is hard, strong and characteristically, is rich and deep. Not surprisingly, the furniture is expensive, but it appreciates, its value grows and it seems to last for generations. Typically, such furniture is handed down through families and is prized. Our challenge therefore, is to produce children who are more like the cedar tree than the soft pine. But it takes nurturing and it takes effort, and it takes time.

If you bring children into the world, understand quite clearly that there are responsibilities and duties, that it is darn hard work.

Let me hasten to add though, that it is also one of the most fulfilling jobs and one of the most enriching experiences. It can be the best harvest.

CHAPTER 1 SUMMARY

Everyone's an Expert

Parenting is Hard Work

Where Do We Learn This Parenting Thing?
The answer is always the same: *from our own parents.*

"Like Father like Son"?
Many of us decide that because we were raised in a particular way that we will not follow suit with our own children. Sometimes this works and sometimes it doesn't.

Then There's the Mix
What complicates the issue even more for parenting is that our partner brings to our relationship a different set of parenting principles based on what he or she received as they were growing up.

The Rules have Changed
You've probably heard someone say recently, "It's all changed since my day". Indeed, they would be right. It has all changed. And that makes the job of parenting even more difficult.

Thou Shalt not Smack or Spank
In many places, the government has enforced the notion that "thou shalt not smack or spank." If we can't smack or spank any longer, what are we supposed to do?

Your Child has "Rights"

Within the education sector too, there has been some social engineering that has been introduced into the school curriculum with the notion that children have "rights." In other words, they do not have to do what mother and father say.

No Training Courses

It seems incredible that the two most basic and important roles that sustain and underpin our whole community, that of being married or a permanent partner, and that of being a parent, involve no real training or instruction at all.

No Training Manuals

When I bought a new washing machine, there was a comprehensive manual that told me everything I needed to know about the appliance. When each of my three children were born, there was no such training manual. There was nothing.

No Short-Cuts & No Immediate Harvest

There is no fast track. No quick recipes. No microwaving to produce the result; instead, it is a long slow bake.

It is also important to understand that there is no immediate harvest. There are countless hours, days and weeks of toiling the soil, seeding and fertilizing, cultivating for weeds and constant overseeing before finally, the grains have matured and the harvest begins.

CHAPTER 2

THE TWO WHEELS OF PARENTING

Start Out With the End in Mind

This famous phrase by Dr Stephen Covey in relation to personal development fits with our own parenting: "Start out with the end in mind." Ask yourself what you really want for your children. How do you want them to be? What are you aiming for? What are your goals for your children?

As parents, you need to be clear about this and you need to write it down. It is simply not good enough to have some general notion in your head about how you'd like it all to end up. It is too important a question not to be addressed seriously.

What Do You Really Want for Your Children?

I have asked this question numerous times in the workshops that I have run for parents.

The answers have been varied, but consistently included those below on the next page.

> ### What do you want for your children?
>
> ✓ **Confidence**
> ✓ **Self-worth**
> ✓ **To be caring**
> ✓ **Happiness**
> ✓ **To be resilient**
> ✓ **Balance in life**
> ✓ **Take risks**
> ✓ **Positive attitude**
> ✓ **Independence**
> ✓ **Be self-reliant**
> ✓ **To have peace**
> ✓ **Self-esteem**
> ✓ **Sense of achievement**
> ✓ **To feel fulfilled**

I'm sure you can add to the list yourself and put down a few more that you might like for your children. If so, write them in the spaces below.

Your list:

....

....

....

....

....

....

Know what you want for your children. Get it clear.

Make sure that as parents you both agree on what you want. Make sure that you are both heading for the same goals and that these goals are very clear and specific; not vague or ambiguous.

"If you don't know where you are going, how can you expect to get there?"

(Darryl Cross)

These characteristics, attributes, values or qualities are the sorts of things that all parents really want for their children. They are universal characteristics and attributes. There is nothing unusual about them.

What is unusual is that although most parents want these kinds of things for their children, they never really sit down and work out how these kinds of attributes can actually be imparted, taken on board or integrated by their offspring.

In other words, there is little doubt that parents want the best for their children and they want the kinds of things that are listed above. Somehow or other though, they must believe that their children will miraculously pick up these particular characteristics, because the sad fact is that parents do not actually sit down and work out how these will be communicated and taught to their children.

How do you actually give your children self-confidence?
How do you teach them about having a positive attitude?
How do you train them to believe in themselves?
How do you let them know about the importance of taking risks at times?
How do you teach them to be independent and self-reliant?

These are critical questions.

The answers to these kinds of questions have to be known. Don't leave it to guesswork. As parents, not only do you have to work out where you are headed and what you want for your children, but you also have to work out how you are going to get there.

This is what this book is all about.

Interestingly, there was a group who researched this whole question of what parents need to do to be "strong, effective parents" and give their children the kinds of things that are important in life.

They came up with the following list:
- Monitor what their children watch on TV
- Check how the internet is being used
- Say no to obscene CDs
- Check where the children are after school and on weekends
- Expect, and are told, the truth about where children go when out at night
- Impose a curfew and make sure it is enforced
- Closely follow children's academic performance
- Let children know that they would be extremely upset if drugs like marijuana were used
- Turn off the TV and sit down as a family over dinner
- Expect children to do jobs around the house
- Have an adult present when children get home from school

(Based on Research by the National Centre on Addiction and Substance Abuse at Columbia University as reported in the *Herald Sun*, 27 March, 2001)

The Power of Modeling

The old adage "do as I say, not as I do" does not hold up at all in parenting. It washes thin. It does **not** work.

For the first few years of life when the basic personality is being laid down, children are watching and observing their

The Two Wheels of Parenting

parents, how they are and how they act. In the very early years, when children cannot yet understand spoken language, they rely on sight and touch in particular. They are keen observers and they pick up the vibes.

> *"Children seldom misquote you. In fact, they usually repeat word for word what you shouldn't have said."*
>
> (Author unknown)

In fact, I have a very strong belief that they are definitely picking up the "vibes" while they are still in the womb where they can hear what is going on outside the womb and sense the mother's moods, emotions and temperament as well as listen to the sound of her voice and the way she says it.

If it is true that children are keen observers and that up until about four years of age, they have observed their parents for around 17,500 hours, then it is probably fair to say that they do not forget what they see.

Your modeling as parents is critical.

> **Someone once calculated that up until a child is about 4 years of age, they have observed their parents for 17,500 hours.**

What children observe over time, they do not forget.

As many parents have told me in my office, in moments of crisis when the pressure is on, they resort to those behaviors that they didn't want to use: those behaviors that were just like their **own** mother or father; those behaviors that they declared they **never** wanted to do with their own children.

For example, they didn't want to rant or rave, scream and yell like their own father or mother might have done, or worse still, be demanding or critical, fault finding and nit-picking, moody, sarcastic or aggressive. Whether they like it or not, the modeling of their own parents was profound. It was imprinted. It sits in the subconscious and gets automatically activated whether they like it or not.

"Children are natural mimics. They act like their parents in spite of every attempt to teach them good manners."

(Author unknown)

So, what does this mean?
- if you want your children to not fly off the handle and to be more calm and rational,
- if you want your children to clean up and be tidy,
- if you want your children not to abuse alcohol in adolescence,
- if you want your children to look after their possessions,
- if you want your children to read or be interested in learning,
- if you want your children to set goals and reach them,
- if you want your children to handle money wisely,
- if you want your children to drive appropriately,
- if you want your children to be open and honest in their communications instead of resorting to backbiting or gossip and manipulation,

....then you have to **show** them the way.

Don't be a parent who sets a double standard and gives confusing messages. On the one hand you tell your child to grow up and be more mature, while on the other hand, you are ranting and raving like a child yourself.

> **Walk the talk, don't just talk the walk!**

On the one hand, you tell your children and adolescents to drive carefully, but on the other hand, you take risks and you speed. On the one hand, you preach the value of education and how your child must do his homework, but you haven't been near a book yourself, done any training courses or shown a willingness to learn a new skill. On the one hand, you constantly nag about your child cleaning up, but you leave your dishes and cups in the family room or on the kitchen sink for someone else to clean up. **Be congruent to your message.**

There is no substitute for appropriate modeling. It is the powerhouse. Words are cheap. Actions count.

The Two Wheels

What we are trying to do with our children is to love them to pieces; love them unconditionally.

What is unconditional love? It is very difficult at times to put into action, but it involves **loving the child for who she is** regardless of her actions or behavior. It is about listening and understanding, supporting and encouraging. It is about praising and appreciating. It is about nurturing, mentoring and coaching. It is about demonstrating your affection with hugs and kisses and telling your child that you love her.

At the same time though, we are responsible for our children and their welfare, and so we need to **provide guidelines and rules** as a way of assisting them. It is important to outline the boundaries for how we and they act and behave. Everyone needs to know the boundaries and our children are no different.

So, how do these two work together?

How does unconditional love on the one hand, coupled with setting boundaries and rules on the other, actually go together?

Is it a possible or is it an impossible task? In fact, it really is a bit like riding a bicycle.

You need to have both wheels functioning really well in order to arrive at your destination.

Both wheels need to be straight, have good tread, and be pumped.

How Problems Arise with Children

There are **three main scenarios** though, where problems seem to arise with children when these "wheels" are out of balance, very wobbly or nonexistent. For example, the love becomes conditional or the boundaries and rules become extreme. Let me explain further.

1. Wobbly Love, and No Rules Wheel

This is the case where the parents are very well-meaning and loving, but are actually spoiling their child.

The parents are constantly giving of their time and of their money and there seem to be no bounds. They are constantly putting themselves out for their children, but ask for nothing in return. They are constantly digging deep into their pockets and showering their children with gifts, treats, holidays, good times and nice clothes, but ask for nothing in return.

These parents are afraid that somehow, if they draw a line in the sand or make a rule, or make a request, that their child is going to hate them or leave home or run away or be upset, or, throw a temper tantrum. These parents are timid and frightened that their own children won't love them or like them. They believe that their children will love them on the condition that they keep giving them things and giving in to them. These parents are frightened of conflict or any disharmony, however slight.

These parents may have come from an abusive background themselves and decided that in no way did they want to treat their own children in the way that they were treated. Perhaps these parents are just very well-intentioned and doing their level best to be loving parents, but have gone overboard with it all.

There is no doubt that they are "loving." But they have got it wrong. Sadly wrong.

It is wrong because there are no limits. There are no guidelines. There are no rules. There are no routines. There are no household chores. There is no accountability. There is nothing coming back from the child. There are no good habits being established. No lessons about how life is really lived. No lessons about how to be independent and responsible in life.

The parents keep giving and giving and the child keeps taking and taking.

The child learns to be demanding; very demanding. If the child does not get what he or she wants, then typically there is World War III, which might be reflected in temper tantrums, yelling abuse at the parents, screaming, slamming doors, breaking things and generally being disruptive.

Of course, usually the parents give in and the child learns to manipulate the household and learns that life is all about taking. If he does not get what he wants, he throws a tantrum.

> Ralph and Janet came to see me because they were simply exhausted in managing their only child. Jason was 8 years old (going on 28 years old).
>
> He was the son that these parents had always wanted. Clearly they loved him. And clearly, they were doing all they could to please this son and make his life enjoyable.
>
> They felt that as good parents they should be there constantly attending to his needs, entertaining him and ensuring that his life was as comfortable as possible. Needless to say, there were few if any boundaries or rules and needless to say, Jason did not lack for anything in terms of toys and clothes or outings.
>
> Of course, Jason had developed into a demanding, verbally manipulative young man. He knew how to take, take, take. This child who had been their dream was turning into a nightmare. The parents were emotionally and physically drained.

Sadly, this child becomes what has been known as **"a spoilt brat."** We see it all too often. Sadly, this demanding spoiled child moves **into adolescence** and the problems exacerbate. The lack of respect for the parents gets worse. The conflict and arguments get worse. The demands get bigger. There are demands for the best in designer label clothes, for the best in sound systems, for the overseas school trips, for the latest in information technology and gadgets. The adolescent demands money for his or her social life. The parents become despairing.

Their golden-haired child, who they had always excused as "spirited" or "strong-willed," has now become a major problem. The parents are at a loss as to what to do. But typically they still give. They buy a car for the adolescent and then threaten to take it away because the adolescent abuses the vehicle and drives irresponsibly, but then they don't follow through. The home becomes a five-star hotel where the adolescent just checks in now and again. In a sense it's an enviable lifestyle.

The adolescent gets everything that he or she wants and has one or two slaves on hand, called parents, who do all the cooking, cleaning, washing, ironing and domestics. The parents inevitably wish that the child would just leave home, but feel guilty for thinking so. They have created a monster, but only a few brave parents could ever say this out loud.

Sadly, this demanding, spoiled child moves **into adulthood** and believes the world owes him or her a living. They always look for the easy track, the shortcut. They look for the hand-out. What they can get, not give. They continue to take. They are difficult to work with because they believe the world should be centered around them. They are high maintenance. The world is supposed to care for their every need and whim. They want things their way. They want people to give into them.

They are difficult to manage **in the workplace**. They create lots of conflict because they find it difficult to work with others. They have always had it their way. They do not work well in teams. Sometimes you see it because they are the loudmouths and very demanding. Sometimes they are seen as the bully or the dictator at work. Sometimes they are the "sniper" at work who gossips and manipulates others. Sometimes they are just seen as the person around whom everyone "walks on eggshells" for fear of an outburst, a verbal tirade or a temper tantrum.

Sadly too, if this spoilt child moves into adulthood and does not break the cycle of living that they are in, subconsciously, they simply seek a partner in life who will continue to be their "slave" and predictably, the cycle continues on. The person never really connects with others, never knows how to really love, never gets in touch with themselves and never finds their real purpose. They typically end up isolated and certainly miserable and unhappy. The script had been set from early days.

2. Bumpy Rules Wheel, and No Love Wheel

This is the case where the parents might again be well-meaning, but there are too many rules, too many restrictions and too tight a rein.

Typically, this is usually the case where one or both parents have had a very restrictive and severe upbringing themselves. They may have had parents who were not loving and were seen as verbally or physically abusive, cold and distant.

Unfortunately, they don't break out of this family circle and simply continue to hand down the poor parenting skills that they have seen their own parents model.

Sadly, they don't know any other way. Sadly, they are not in touch enough with themselves to look at how they are interacting within their family and with their children. Sadly, they get locked into punitive harsh measures as a way of trying to raise their children.

> Perhaps one of the worst cases I can ever recall was when I was in charge of a unit for children with severe behavior problems at a Children's Hospital. This was a withdrawal unit where children were taken out of the traditional classroom at their own schools because their problems were so severe and were taken daily to a unit that was associated with the hospital.
>
> The unit consisted of a multidisciplinary team of teachers, social workers, psychologists, occupational therapists and backup administrative staff.
>
> The children would attend there for one or two school terms, on a full-time basis in a classroom setting, while intensive therapy was also undertaken with the child and the family. Intervention with the child's school was also undertaken to prepare for the child's return.
>
> I remember this young 9-year old boy with blonde hair and a pleasant round face who sat in my office. He wasn't very communicative.
>
> In fact, he was largely sullen and withdrawn. It was after about six or seven weeks of him attending at our unit that he became slightly more open and communicative.
>
> It was then that his story started to emerge. His stepfather was a grotesque man. This man would punish this boy by beating him with a garden hose.
>
> When the boy was in bed asleep the stepfather would come in and rip him out of the bed and throw him against the wall. If he really wanted to punish this young man, he would lock him in the dark cellar, which was a haven for rats.

Of course, this is an extreme example of what being "harsh" is all about.

Many children, teenagers and adults however, tell me with some sadness or anger about their own upbringing.

They say things like:

"My father was so strict...and he never told me that he loved me."

"The other kids at school thought I was a "nerd" because I was never allowed to go out like they were."

"My father was always criticizing me and putting me down...I don't think I ever heard him say anything positive to me."

"I once overheard my father telling my uncle that he thought I was a "good kid," but never once did he tell me or even suggest that he was proud of me in any way."

"Our house was run like an army camp...Dad used to be in the army."

"If Dad said something in our house everyone jumped, even Mum, because none of us wanted his yelling and abuse."

"We never really had any fun in our family...it was always lots of rules and regulations."

"Mum used to put me down all the time and call me a "slut" or a "whore" if I used to ask if I could go out with a group of my friends to the pictures or go to a party."

"I never heard my mum or dad say that they loved each other and it was only when I was married and on my wedding day that my father gave me a kiss."

"I remember being late home one night and my parents grounded me for six months."

"My parents never let me buy my own clothes or even go shopping with me...they made me dress in what they wanted...and I still remember feeling so embarrassed, even to this day."

If it happens to be one parent who is extremely harsh and punitive, then it may well be that the other parent tries to compensate by being "soft." Of course, this divides the parents and drives a wedge between them. The parents argue about parenting. The more one parent takes the "soft" track, the more the other decides to be harsh and restrictive. The child is caught in between.

This kind of harsh restrictive parenting sabotages self-esteem. It destroys children, some of whom never recover. Typically, this kind of restrictive parenting produces withdrawn or *depressed* children with low self-esteem. Sometimes these children see no way out except suicide. The pain is too great. These children are damaged emotionally and psychologically.

If the child does not become depressed, then the child will become *angry* and act out. At school for example, the child can be aggressive and fight. This child might break things and destroy their own property as well as others, he might lie or cheat or steal, be non-compliant and do not do as asked, be disruptive in class. At home, the child hits back by breaking things and there is a good deal of yelling and screaming and not surprisingly, this leads to physical fights.

As adolescents in this situation, the response can be that they need intensive psychiatric care for an extended period. They may well need to see the school counselor for a good deal of time because they are presenting as depressed or perhaps anxious. Sometimes these adolescents run away. They drop out of school. They feel lost.

Where the parenting is harsh, but not in an extreme sense, there is still low self-esteem and periods of feeling low and feeling lost. There are many adults for example, who for all intents and purposes seem quite capable on the outside, but scratch the surface and underneath there are huge hurts about their own parenting, and about the lack of love and care they received from their parents.

It also needs to be said that the harshness may not necessarily be physical, but could certainly be verbal in the form of criticism or "putdowns." Some people believe that this is worse than physical abuse.

Nevertheless, **the fact remains that finding fault with children, constantly criticizing, showing a lack of love and**

affection, and not telling children that they are loved eats at the heart of self-esteem.

Children who have been on the end of this kind of parenting say as adolescents or adults that they feel inferior, that they feel not good enough, that they never quite measure up.

Not surprisingly, they start a cycle of life that means they might never feel fulfilled, never reach their goals, never know what it is to be their best. They are always on the search for endless love (the love that they never received from their parents).

3. No Love Wheel, and No Rules Wheel

Of all the scenarios, this is the worst. Both wheels have fallen off. It is difficult to ride a bike with no wheels at all!

This is the case of total indifference and of total abdication. **If it sabotages self-esteem to have a harsh and punitive parent, then to have a parent who simply does not care in any way is soul destroying.**

This is the parent who is completely self-centered, who is caught up in their own sense of importance, in their own significance. They have their own life and their own world. Children are often seen as an intrusion into their world and into their life. This may not be said overtly or out loud, but the parent's actions say it clearly. Actions speak louder than words. The children do not count. The children are not wanted.

It is probably true to say that there are **two main types of parents** in this category.

First, there is the *parent* **who has a priority in other directions than family.**

Often these parents are the affluent, wealthy kind (but not necessarily so). It is more important for these parents to be successful in the workplace and to give their time and attention to the work setting.

It is more important for these parents to get the dollars that come out of working in order to afford the prestige cars, the overseas holidays, the luxury dining, the expensive clothes and the lavish entertainment.

It is more important for this parent to attend all the social gatherings including the various fashion or charity shows, the morning or afternoon teas, the exhibitions or first night openings.

It is more important for them to be recognized in their social set than it is to be in touch with their children. It is more important for these parents to be on various committees and boards than it is to be involved in any family conferences or get-togethers.

It is more important for these parents to **feed their ego** than it is to give out to those around them, especially their children.

Second, there are the **parents who are totally lost themselves.**

This might mean that they are in a cycle of poverty, on drugs, unemployed or have a psychiatric diagnosis. They literally have little or no energy for themselves, let alone anyone else in their life. They are not able to care for themselves, let alone their children. They do not know how to love themselves, let alone anyone else around them. They do not know how to feed themselves, let alone nurture their children. They do not know how to take care of their own personal hygiene, let alone keep their children clean and well-dressed. They don't know how to make it to appointments on time, let alone get their children to school on time. Sometimes they are broken individuals. They therefore have little or no hope of being able to fix or help those around them.

In many situations, it also needs to be recognized that this sense of "indifference" on the part of the parents may not be as extreme as I may have painted above.

Perhaps, instead, there is the parent who is simply caught up in his own world who is so intent on trying to get out the door in the morning that he does not attend to the child's needs or show the child how to get ready on time. Perhaps it is the parent who is so concerned with her own issues, thoughts, and feelings, that she does not acknowledge her child, encourage the child, or praise the child.

Nevertheless, the picture is the same. The children do not count. Sometimes too, they are not wanted. They are not loved. They are not on the parents' radar screen.

For example, I have had individuals say the following to me:

"I wish my parents had come to see me play sports on Saturday mornings or come to one of my school plays...they never seemed interested."

"I remember trying really hard and getting A's in my Tenth Grade school report, but Mom and Dad didn't even mention it."

"I never quite knew if my father loved me...he gave me lots of things, but he was always too busy to have any time for me."

"I sometimes wondered if I ran away whether either of my parents would really notice."

"I thought I would shoplift because I figured that was probably one way to get my parents' attention."

"I could do anything I wanted as I was growing up, but I really wished my parents would sometimes stop me from doing all the things that I was doing."

"I spent much of my life just trying to survive...I lived for a while with Grandma...and with some of my friends...and it was really hard."

"My mum was an alcoholic and she had lots of boyfriends at home and I had no idea who my father was...usually it was just my little brother and me...and I looked after him and brought him up."

The Two Wheels of Parenting

> *"My father left years ago and mother was too busy having a good time so I used to climb out of my bedroom window around 2 or 3am and go off and see my friends and do stuff."*

In other words, perhaps we all know of parents who put themselves first, either through choice or through necessity, where clearly, their children do not count.

However, it is also certainly true to say that there are a broad band of parents who might give the impression that they care, but the real agenda is that they have other priorities than their family or their children. Without doubt, children pick this message up. Children have great radar and are champions at picking up the vibes.

Perhaps all of us as parents at some stage are guilty of this kind of "indifference." It is a damaging message. It hits at the souls of our children.

Unconditional Love & Appropriate Rules

The aim of the parent is to ensure that both the wheel of **unconditional love** on the one hand and **control** on the other are fully functioning.

Of course, at times it can be difficult to keep both rolling at once and consistently so. Sometimes we might get a buckle or a flat tire. Occasionally both stop when the chain comes off! Sometimes we get it right as parents and sometimes we get it wrong.

Nevertheless, it should always be our aim to keep both wheels rolling.

Keeping both wheels pumped and in good order is what produces a secure and responsible child.

> **Finding the balance between love and control is what produces secure and responsible children.**

The child who is secure in the love of the parents while at the same time has learned to be responsible through the control and boundaries that have been administered will journey on to become the kind of adult for whom the parents would have wished.

Interestingly, although typically children buck against control, it is my opinion that they actually want such controls, including rules and boundaries.

Believe it or not, such controls allow the child to feel secure and in a sense, to feel "safe."

Of course, **children push against the boundaries and test them, but that really is a way of ensuring that the boundaries are going to hold and that the boundaries will, in fact, keep them "safe"**.

I still well recall the 10-year-old boy who attended the special withdrawal treatment unit attached to the hospital where I was a director.

He came up to me in the playground area and said, "Dr Cross, I really like it when you adults make rules because it makes me feel safe."

I was amazed at his insight.

Out of the mouths of "babes" comes real wisdom.

The Two Wheels of Parenting

But raising secure and responsible children is extremely difficult to achieve through a spontaneous, "fly by the seat of your pants" approach. It just doesn't happen. It has to be thought out with planned strategies.

Sadly, many parents believe that somehow or other, it is just going to happen. Nothing is further from the truth. Nothing just happens.

It has to be planned. Parents have to take time out and sit down with each other and work out how they do this parenting thing.

> **Many parents spend more time planning a weekend barbeque, picnic or outing than they do their parenting.**

Unfortunately, lots of parents spend more time planning a weekend barbecue or holiday than they ever do sitting down and working out their own parenting, and how to achieve a consistent style between both parents with the aim of raising children who are independent and responsible with healthy self-esteem.

The next chapters show one approach to parenting that is planned and purposeful. I have used this approach to instruct and train parents, and it has worked well for over more than a decade and a half.

It is about ensuring that both wheels of "Love" and "Rules" are pumped up and rolling well.

CHAPTER 2 SUMMARY

Start Out With the End in Mind

This famous phrase by Dr Stephen Covey in relation to personal development fits with our own parenting. It is simply not good enough to have some general notions in your head about how you'd like it all to end up.

What Do You Really Want for Your Children?

Know what you want for your children. Get it clear. Make sure that both parents agree on what you both want. Make sure that you are both heading for the same goals and that these goals are very clear and specific and not vague or ambiguous.

The Power of Modeling

The old adage "do as I say, not as I do" does not hold up at all in parenting. It simply does not work.

The Two Wheels

There are two main parameters for raising children: unconditional love and setting rules and boundaries. How does unconditional love on the one hand, coupled with setting boundaries and rules on the other, actually go together?

In fact, it really is a bit like riding a bicycle. You need to have both wheels functioning really well in order to arrive at your destination.

How Problems Arise with Children
There are three main scenarios where problems seem to arise with children. This is when one wheel is not functioning or worse still, when perhaps both wheels are non-existent.

1. Wobbly Love, and No Rules Wheel
This is the case where the parents are very well-meaning and very loving, but they spoil their child. The parents are constantly giving of their time and of their money and there seem to be no boundaries or rules.

2. Bumpy Rules Wheel, and No Love Wheel
This is the case where the parents might again be well-meaning, but there are too many rules, too many restrictions and too tight a rein.

3. No Love Wheel, and No Rules Wheel
Of all the scenarios, this is the worst. This is the case of total indifference. Both wheels have fallen off.

Unconditional Love and Appropriate Rules
The aim of the parent is to ensure that both wheels of unconditional love on the one hand and control on the other are fully functioning.

Of course, at times it can be difficult to keep both rolling at once and consistently so. Sometimes we might get a buckle or a flat tire. Nevertheless, it should always be our aim to keep both wheels rolling.

Keeping both wheels pumped and in good order is what produces a secure and responsible child.

CHAPTER 3

THE LOVE WHEEL

Love being Unconditional

What is unconditional love? What does it really mean to give unconditional love?

This is a difficult call for many people because **much of what we receive in life is conditional**.

For example, we earn an extra badge in boy scouts or girl guides because we have demonstrated a new skill or endeavor, we get put in the higher math class because we demonstrated that we could get consistent A's, we get placed in the senior swimming team because we got our lap times down, we get a raise in pay at work because we have increased our sales figures.

On the other hand, we could get dropped from the top team because our performance has fallen off or we could get demoted or fired because our work performance was significantly down. It's all conditional or dependent on what we do and how we perform.

What is the number one fear among all people (including children, of course)? It's rejection. Why? Because we measure the results of our efforts in terms of whether the world accepts or rejects us.

Unconditional love is **not** about measuring results or how you perform. It is about loving *irrespective* of the results or the performance. It is about loving no matter what.

Here is an exercise for you.

> *Think of all the people in your life who have had the most positive influence in your life. Now, recall one person from that list who has had a profound and positive impact on you.*
>
> - ✓ What did they do?
> - ✓ What did they do that you liked?
> - ✓ What did you feel about yourself when you were with them?
> - ✓ What traits or characteristics did they possess?

I am not sure what your specific answers might be, but when I have asked this question in various coaching workshops that I have run particularly with corporations and government organizations, the kinds of answers that I receive sound something like this:

They:......
- ➢ **listened to me**
- ➢ **encouraged me**
- ➢ **challenged me**
- ➢ **believed in me**
- ➢ **made me feel special**
- ➢ **supported me**
- ➢ **coached me**
- ➢ **told me that they loved me**
- ➢ **gave me special treats**

These people who have had an impact on other's lives vary greatly from teachers, grandparents, current and former bosses, current and former managers, friends, sport coaches to of course, parents.

Ultimately, these special people gave you the greatest gift of all. **They allowed you to believe in yourself.** Surely, this is unconditional love at its very best.

> "It's not who you are that holds you back, it is who you think you are not."
>
> (Author unknown)

Being unconditional, however, is contrary to much of what goes on around us. It sort of goes against everything that we see and hear on a daily basis that is performance or results-oriented. How do we do it then? How do we demonstrate unconditional love?

Actioning Love

Unconditional love is real love in action. It's the "see and do" of love.

There are a number of specific points that need to be understood and taken on board by parents that shows children (and others) that love is unconditional; that they are loved for who they are and that you believe in them – nothing more, nothing less.

1. What is Over, is Over

You can't change what is over. No matter how much you say "I should have...I could have...if only...." it is all history. As the saying goes, "It's no use crying over spilled milk."

If you have said or done something in your parenting that you regret, then leave it behind you. **You can't drive forward while you are busy looking in the rear vision mirror.** You will crash or have an accident if you do that.

Life is about making mistakes and learning from them. Every mistake is an opportunity to learn. There's no point in berating yourself and beating up on yourself as a parent – what does that achieve? How is that supposed to make things better?

> *"Failure is the opportunity to begin again more intelligently."*
>
> (Henry Ford; 1863-1947, USA car manufacturer)

On the other hand, if your child has said or done something that has left you feeling bad and thinking bad thoughts about her, don't harbor grudges.

Don't keep count. Don't keep a scorecard.

Love is about moving on and starting a new moment because that's what it is, new.

By the way, children tend not to keep count or keep score because they really only have "now" time; if they don't keep count, why should you?

2. Forgiveness is the Fragrance

Mark Twain once wrote, *"Forgiveness is the fragrance that the violet sheds on the heel that has crushed it."* Forgiveness is love in action. It is the "see and do" of love.

Consider a snake bite – in the same way, **refusing to forgive your children is like venom in the thoughts that you carry with you and it ultimately destroys you.**

The Love Wheel

Here's how it is.

We make up rules inside our heads about how our children **should** react and behave towards us and others. When they "break" those rules, we get upset (or annoyed, resentful, frustrated, angry etc). We play it cool and are aloof, we get angry and blow our stack, we are short and impatient with our children like we're on a short fuse.

> *"Forgiveness does not change the past, but it does enlarge the future."*
>
> (Author unknown)

But really, in a nutshell, feeling resentful or badly towards our children for breaking our rules is ridiculous. Somehow or other, we believe that we can punish others by refusing to forgive them. *"If I don't forgive you, you suffer."*

Know what? **Actually, it's us that suffers**. We're the ones who feel tense, it's our stomach that churns, we're the ones who lose sleep, we're the ones who feel fatigued, we're the ones who get headaches, we're the ones who feel miserable.

What's the Answer? This is not a cop-out, but the answer is within you.

Don't punish yourself by trying to punish your children in this way. It's futile. It's senseless. Give up trying to make them feel badly or feel poorly. Take charge of yourself. Let it all go. Silently forgive.

On the other hand, it may indeed be you as a parent who needs to ask for forgiveness. In this case, you need to be courageous enough to say those two little words, *"I'm sorry."* Also adding some words to the effect that you will try and not let that happen again or you will try to work on your outbursts or behavior would be entirely appropriate.

3. Think Positively about Your Child

I have heard it said that some children are easy to love because they are so "cute" or "pretty" or "smart." I have also heard parents say that they have a strong affection for a particular child because he or she reminds them of someone such as a grandfather, grandmother or uncle or perhaps they are a "chip off the old block" or "look just like their mother."

Irrespective, **it is important for parents to understand the power of positive thinking. Try to always see your children in a positive light**. Have positive thoughts about them. Remind yourself how fortunate you are to have these children. They are a gift to you. Thinking positively about your children means that you will then feel positive towards them and act positively towards them.

In a way, it's like building up an emotional bank account with them. They are always in the "black" with you in that you always see them positively rather than being in the "red" with you where you are short on emotion, lack tolerance and lack patience.

See them as special and tell them so. Because they are.

When was the last time you told your children that they were special, that they were important to you and that you really loved them? Do your children know how important they are to you?

4. Listen, Really, Really Listen

Really listening is really loving. It is definitely love in action. It is certainly something that takes time, but really listening to your children is a way of really affirming who they are and what they are about.

The Love Wheel

The one area that children consistently complain about is that their parents do not seem to listen to them. Whether this is perception or reality has little to do with the issue. Perception *is* reality and if children believe that their parents are not taking the time to listen to them, then they would rightfully also perceive that they do not count, that their parents do not respect them, and that they are not important.

Did you know that there are actually **5 levels of listening**? They are as follows:

(1) **Ignoring** (this is particularly hurtful)
(2) **Pretending** "Yeah. Uh-huh. Right." (but you're really elsewhere in your thoughts and pre-occupied with other "important" things)
(3) **Selective Listening** Hearing only certain parts of the conversation (you focus on what **you** want to focus on)
(4) **Active Listening** Paying attention to the words being said and being able to recite them back if necessary
(5) **Empathic Listening** This is listening with the intent to really understand and comprehend and where you not only understand the content of what was said, but you understand the feeling and emotion that went with it

Now, no prizes for guessing which levels we use almost all the time with our children. You got it. Level 1, 2 or 3. (And sadly, what levels do we use with our marriage partner or permanent partner? – yes, you got it again! – Level 1, 2 or 3.)

Not only are our actions telling our children that they are unimportant and that they do not count enough for us to listen to them, but more particularly, we are also being very poor role models in teaching our children effective communication.

Have you ever had the experience of having someone tell you that they are a really good listener or that they are good with people, but within a very short while in conversation, you realize that quite the opposite is true?

I remember running a therapy group a long time back and one woman in the group introduced herself and indicated that she felt one of her strengths was being "a good listener," but in the very next group exercise, she could not remember the name of her partner, although she had just been talking to her, nor could she remember anything about her!

Why do we so often think that we can listen, but really we do not? The answer lies in the fact that because we have ears, we automatically assume that we can listen. Wrong. Having ears and hearing is not listening. Listening is not the same as hearing. "Hearing" is really a passive act which really does not require you to participate. In contrast, "listening" is an active act which demands your real attention.

> "You have been given two ears and one mouth...and you should use them in that proportion."
>
> (Author unknown)

You know as well as I do that if you stop and think about it, you can hear every word of the statement and yet have not paid an atom of attention to it. You heard with your ears, but you did not listen.

What Listening Is Not: "Listening" is **not** any one of the following:

1. **Maintaining a polite silence:** listening does not mean simply maintaining a polite silence while you are rehearsing in your head the speech or lecture you are going to make the next time your child stops talking and you can grab a conversational opening.

2. **Mowing others down:** listening does not mean waiting alertly for the flaws in your child's arguments so that later you can mow him or her down.

The Love Wheel

3. **Having all the answers and giving advice:** listening does not mean that you are supposed to come up with all the necessary answers to problems or issues or be especially knowledgeable, expert, wise and sophisticated. As parents, you are human too and children need to know that you don't know everything (even though you'd probably like to).

4. **Giving inappropriate minimal responses:** listening is not simply a case of saying "I see" or "yes" or "uh-huh" at various pauses or at specific times in the conversation when you think it looks or sounds appropriate to do so.

5. **Playing "psychiatrist":** listening is not trying to be insightful and interpretive and kind of "big dealing" yourself by being in touch with the latest theories on human dynamics, child behavior and personal development.

6. **Parroting:** listening is not regurgitating back to your child word for word what you have directly heard (like an audio recorder play-back does) nor does it mean being like a "parrot."

7. **Automatic skill:** listening is not something that comes naturally or automatically, where everyone is just born with the skill and everyone has an in-built ability to be able to listen and communicate with others around them.

What Listening Is:

1. **Empathy:** listening is being able to show empathy for a child, which means experiencing with him or her what they feel and think. This means entering actively and imaginatively into their situation and trying to understand a frame of reference and a perspective different from your own.

   It means not only hearing the words, but picking up the feeling tones, even perhaps the meaning that might be somewhat hidden for your child. It means tuning in to the body language as well as the words. Can we sense the shape of our children's inner worlds; can we put ourselves in their shoes and appreciate what it is like to be them?

In the novel "To Kill a Mockingbird," listening appropriately is described as the ability to jump inside the skin of the other person and walk around and see the world through the eyes of the other. Do we have both the desire and the talent to do this for our children?

2. **Asking questions:** a good listener does not merely remain silent, but is prepared to ask questions without any hint of skepticism or challenge or hostility (whether in wording or non-verbally). Such questions need to be clearly motivated by genuine curiosity about your child's view on things and as such, these could be called "questions for clarification." These questions simply request more information (e.g. "Can you tell me more about that?" "Can you say that again?").

3. **Giving feedback:** as an effective listener, you must communicate to your child that he or she has been heard, and importantly, this needs to be done in a non-judgmental, accepting, non-evaluative and caring way. Therefore, saying things like, "What you are really saying is....." or "Sounds like what you've said....." allows your child to know if you are "on target" and are correct in what you consider you have just heard.

4. **A learned skill:** it is not innate, but is an acquired skill that has to be practiced and practiced and worked at (like many other skills in life).

Redemptive and Creative

Being able to intensively listen to your children is like giving them a gift. It is truly redemptive to them i.e. it lifts them up, it redeems, it liberates them, it compensates for what might have gone on before.

Redemptive because when someone really hears us and sensitively understands, it frees us from the fear of ourselves and our inadequacies and feelings of lack of self-worth. We kind of say, "Well, if they have seen me for what I really am and still are prepared to talk to me and like me, then maybe I'm not so bad after all; maybe I don't have to hide anymore."

Redemptive because we become more whole and re-own those parts of us that we have previously shut away. Creative because it unleashes new energy in us to grow; it encourages us to move on and continue to find ourselves and grapple with life.

Listening is a very real gift. We all have the ability to use it if we wish. Practice it and its power will be absolutely profound. Are you using your gift with your children? When was the last time that you listened, really, really listened?

5. Having Fun and Giving Special Treats

Love in action is having fun with your children. It is about enjoying one another's company. It is about laughing, messing around and generally having a good time. When was the last time that you actually took time to have fun?

Of course, the "fun" could **be organized** such as a day outing to a theme park, the beach, the local swimming pool, or a picnic. This "fun" time is really just for you and your children. Don't ask along the neighbor's children or your nieces or nephews or your children's friends because you only end up being a babysitter and it really does little to directly assist your relationship with your own children. Instead, sit down with your own children and plan out what both you and they would like to do. What are the options? What are the choices? It doesn't have to cost money. It could be a walk to the local playground where they try out the equipment for an hour or so. It could be a bike ride or a walk to the local park.

But fun is also about **being spontaneous**. It is about suggesting things on the spur of the moment. Such adds variety and spice to life – for adults and children alike.

When was the last time that out of the blue, you suggested a trip to McDonald's or Hungry Jacks or a walk to the local shop for an ice cream or a game of football in the backyard or flying the kite in the local park?

Love in action is also about giving treats. Special surprises. It might be making your child's favorite milk drink or pulling out a candy bar for no other reason than it is a treat and you feel like spoiling your child and making her feel special.

6. Spending Time with your Children

Giving your children your time is showing that you care and that they count.

In this day and age, time is at a premium.

How often do we hear people saying that they "don't have enough time." We all have enough time. **It is really a matter of how we prioritize that time**. We all have 168 hours in a week. You can't get any more or any less hours —
that's it. How we use those hours, though, is up to us to decide.

In a busy world, it is easy for our children to get the impression that we do not have enough time for them and that they are not important enough for us to be sharing our moments with them. They pick up our vibes, they recognize our non- verbal's and they hear our comments.

Of course, we are busy and we are often stretched for time.

Further, we are not there for our children's beck and call to jump immediately when we are summoned. Instead, it is more about negotiating our time and arranging time together for things like homework, attending the school play or musical, watching school sports on the weekend and perhaps just doing stuff together around the house.

It is about recognizing when your child wants assistance, while you on the other hand, had other plans in mind or other jobs to do. You can come to an arrangement together about that time or indeed, you may put aside your own needs to attend to those of your child.

What you do with your time sends a powerful message to your children about how important they are in your life.

> *"The best thing to spend on your children is time."*
>
> (Author unknown)

CHAPTER 3 SUMMARY

Love being Unconditional

Unconditional love is **not** about measuring results or how you perform.

It is about loving irrespective of the results or the performance. It is about loving no matter what.

Actioning Love

Unconditional love is real love in action. It's the "see and do" of love.

There are a number of specific points that need to be understood and taken on board by parents that shows children (and others) that love is unconditional; that they are loved for who they are and that you believe in them.

1. What is Over, is Over

If you have said or done something in your parenting that you regret, then leave it behind you. You can't drive forward while you are busy looking in the rear vision mirror.

On the other hand, if your child has said or done something that has left you feeling bad and thinking bad thoughts about him or her, don't harbor grudges.

Love is about moving on and starting a new moment because that's what it is, new.

2. Forgiveness is the Fragrance
Forgiveness is love in action. It is the "see and do" of love.

3. Think Positively about Your Child
It is important for parents to understand the power of positive thinking. Try to always see your children in a positive light.

Thinking positively about your children means that you will then feel positive towards them and act positively towards them.

4. Listen, Really, Really Listen
Really listening is really loving. It is definitely love in action.

It is certainly something that takes time, but really listening to your children is a way of affirming who they are and what they are about.

5. Having Fun and Giving Special Treats
Love in action is having fun with your children. It is about enjoying one another's company. It is about laughing, messing around and generally having a good time.

6. Spending Time with Your Children
Giving your children your time is showing that you care and that they count.

What you do with your time sends a powerful message to your children about how important they are in your life.

CHAPTER 4

THE RULES WHEEL

A second important wheel on the journey of parenting is how to set rules and boundaries.

Of course, it is assumed that we already surround our child with **unconditional love, which is** designed to enhance their self-esteem.

Rules and boundaries without love can be punitive, put children down, sap their energies and cause significant fracturing to their self-confidence levels.

Further, it is also assumed that we already **encourage our children's talents and abilities** in order to give them additional self-confidence. With unconditional love plus encouragement and support in their talents and strengths, the stage is now set to put in place the rules and boundaries.

Putting the rules and boundaries ahead of love and encouragement only serves to throw you and your children out of balance.

First comes love, then comes encouragement and praise and then the rules.

Once the scene is set with an atmosphere of love, the task is to set boundaries in which your children can live and move and in which they can keep themselves safe and secure.

Step 1: Set the Rules

Generally speaking, **there are two major problems in families when it comes to rules or setting boundaries.**

Firstly, often there are none. In other words, there are no firm rules, guidelines or understanding about what needs to happen when. There are no responsibilities that the child is given to help the family function as a whole. There are no clear expectations about what needs to happen and how it is supposed to happen.

Parents have this notion that somehow or other, the child is simply going to "catch on."

Secondly, if there are any rules, then typically they are vague. For example, as we drive off to visit Grandma or other relatives, we tell our children sitting in the back seat to be "good." What on earth does that mean? Take a poll of your children and you may find that in one instance it might mean not sitting in Grandma's favorite chair or perhaps it might mean not interrupting the adults when they are talking or perhaps it might mean not running along Grandma's hallway or it might mean not fighting with their baby brother or sister when at Grandma's.

One main reason we have so much difficulty in the family is that the rules are generally not clear. Consequently, we make it difficult for ourselves if the rules are vague and wishy-washy. This means you can be sure we will have endless debates and arguments over the *interpretation of the rules* because they are not specific and are not clear. In fact, we often end up in uproar over what we all thought the rules meant.

The Rules Wheel

> *"If the rules on the road were as vague as they are in the family, we'd all be too scared to drive."*
>
> (Darryl Cross)

Let's look at what happens using roads as an analogy.

How would you feel if we had no rules for our road usage or if the rules we did have were vague and ambiguous? It's bad enough on our roads out there even with fairly tight rules. Without them, I don't think that I'd venture out on the road at all. I'd be too scared to drive!

What would it be like if the road rules we had were vague?

For example, what if there were no speed signs at all and the sign on the side of the road simply said "Drive Carefully." So that means that you can drive at 60mph (100 km/hour) through a main city street and if the traffic policeman pulls you over and says you were driving too fast or not driving carefully, you no doubt would retort that, of course, you were being careful. You could well end up having a heated discussion about the interpretation of what "careful" really meant.

Step 2: Set the Right Rules

How do we know which rules we should put in place? How do we work out which rules to have?

Let's go back to the road analogy.

Why is it that some corners and intersections have traffic lights and others do not? Answer: because more accidents and injuries occur on those corners and intersections than on any others.

So what does this mean for the family? It means that **wherever the family constantly has "accidents" or "crashes," this is a sure sign that some "traffic lights" or rules need to be put up or put in place.**

Whenever we are having constant drama or turmoil or having fairly constant arguments and disagreements, it is probably because we either have no rules, or any rules that are in place are vague and ambiguous.

This is an important principle in any family. Wherever there is an "accident" or "hot-spot" area, parents need to do themselves a service and immediately put in a rule. It's really commonsense, isn't it?

If you had a dangerous intersection near your home where there were relatively constant accidents, then you would no doubt lobby your local politician or councilor to fix up the intersection and ensure that it was safe (especially if *you* had to cross the intersection frequently).

So it is with families. Work out where you have most arguments and most conflict and see what rule you can put in place, as an important first step in bringing some order and some harmony back into the family.

> **There is an important principle that parents need to always remember. Whenever there is a "hot-spot" area in the family or an area of constant conflict, parents need to put in a rule.**

My own clinical observation however, says that that there are **basically four major "accident" or "crash" areas in almost every family**.

The Rules Wheel

Of course, it can vary somewhat between families, but overall, there is an overwhelming consensus that says without fail, most families will crash at four particular "intersections."

What are those four areas?

1. The Morning Routine

Without fail, getting up in the morning, having breakfast and getting ready to leave by a particular time in order to get to school on time is generally a danger zone for most parents and children. If there is more than one child in the family, the problem is only accentuated. This is especially so if one child seems to understand the routine relatively well while the other child seems to have little idea of how to manage the routine and get out of the house by the appointed time.

This problem in the morning is also further exacerbated because somehow or other, the child or children seem to lack what we fondly call "organizational skills."

In other words, being able to find all their pieces of clothing including their shoes and socks, and being able to put them on neatly, being able to locate their pencil case and their books, including their diary, and being able to pack their bag seems to be beyond some children. This thing called organization seems to have completely eluded them.

Incidentally, if you look closely, it can often run in families and although the children themselves may be naturally untidy and not particularly organized, it may also be that they have a parent who certainly models similar for them. In this instance, it is the parent who needs to set some rules for themselves and who needs to demonstrate how it is all done.

Furthermore, the drama can be accentuated because not only do the children have to be out the door by a particular time, but also, if the parent or parents happen to be working, they also need to be out of the door at a specific time.

Chaos and guerrilla warfare can reign supreme. This is the time when voice volumes reach their peak and generally speaking, parents start to rant and rave.

- *"Will you get out of bed! How many times do I have to call you?"*
- *"For crying out loud, turn off that television and get ready!"*
- *"How long does it take you to eat your cornflakes?"*
- *"I've got no idea where you put your shoes last night!"*
- *"How do I know where your school hat is....you took it off, so you find it!"*
- *"What do you mean you're still not dressed...you've been in that bedroom for 20 minutes at least!"*
- *"What are you doing just sitting on that bed...you're supposed to be getting ready!"*
- *"Hurry up in that bathroom...there's more than one of us that has to use it!"*
- *"Your brother is always ready on time, why can't you be?"*
- *"Hurry up or we'll be late again!"*

The deadlines for being out the door and into the car or the deadlines for catching the bus or the train can create stress and pressure which means that many parents openly confess to "losing it."

2. The Evening Routine

You guessed it. At the other end of the day, there is the evening routine which really starts once your child comes home from school and ends once your child is in bed with the light out.

At this "intersection," crashes occur almost from the time the child comes home from school and enters the front door. There is a lot that happens in this period with homework, dinner, bedtime and all the other "stuff" that occurs.

The Rules Wheel

- "Stop running into the house and leaving the door open!"
- "Don't just drop your bag in the corner there!"
- "How many times have I told you to put your bag away!"
- "No, you can't turn on the television until you've changed out of your uniform."
- "No, you can't go out to play until you've done your homework."
- "Stop annoying your brother!"
- "How many times do I have to tell you to get off that computer and do your homework."
- "How many times do I have to tell you that it is your job to feed the dog?"
- "How many times do I have to call you to come to the table for dinner?"
- "We go through this every night...why don't you just get into the shower the first time I ask you to?"
- "Look, we've already had three stories...now it's time for bed."
- "Go to sleep...no...you can't have another glass of water!"

It's like the parent is constantly directing traffic and handing out infringement notices! It is draining and wearing.

Not only does the parent have to nag to get things done, but the parent also has to make sure that the family functions, that meals are prepared, that the place is tidied up and that the parent has some personal time later in the night (if they're not too exhausted).

Again, the situation is exacerbated if there is more than one child and exacerbated still further if there is only one parent, either because the other parent is still at work or otherwise engaged or because it is a single parent family.

It is not surprising that by the end of the day, parents are generally exhausted and flop into bed.

The depressing part is that it happens all over again the next day.

3. Children Fighting or Not Getting On

Of course, this does not really apply if there is only one child in the family, except to say that this whole area of "sharing" for a single child generally rears its head when the child's friends come over to play or, the cousins drop in to visit. It is then that the issue of sharing toys and getting on with others comes to the fore for one-child families.

However, if there is more than one child, then clearly this is a "crash" area where the parent seems to continually play the role of referee or umpire.

Of course, the major problem with being an umpire or a referee is that neither side likes you! You can't win. No matter what you do, either one side or the other will either cheer you or boo you and frequently, both will boo you. Lovely, isn't it. You never end up pleasing both parties and generally speaking, both parties will argue the toss about your decision.

Furthermore, the children often keep reminding you how "unfair" your decision was.

- "How many times have I told you to leave your sister alone!"
- "Okay, who did that?"
- "Did you kick your brother as he walked past?"
- "So, whose turn is it really on the computer?"
- "What do you mean 'he always gets to watch his TV programs and you never get to watch any of yours'?"
- "Will you two stop that!"
- "Stop doing that...someone is going to get hurt, you know."
- "How many times have I told you that you've got to share?"
- "Let your brother have a turn on your Nintendo...He's not going to hurt it."
- "What do you mean 'he's looking at you funny'?"

The Rules Wheel

> - "For goodness sake, can't you two just sit on the sofa without annoying each other?"
> - "What do you mean 'he's over on your side of the seat'?"
> - "Your brother says you're cheating and you won't go "out"...is that right?"
> - "What do you mean 'he's eaten all the chips and you haven't had any'?"
> - "Don't be silly, your ice cream is the same size as his...now just eat it!"

You know the scenario. Somehow or other children just don't seem to be able to get on.

Ironically though, many parents tell me that although their children will fight like cat and dog, if someone outside the family (e.g. other children or neighbors) picks on one of them, their children come together and support each other like there was no tomorrow! When the chips are down, they are certainly there for each other.

Most of the time however, parents complain that they tend to annoy each other, deliberately antagonize each other, and almost go out of their way to irritate the other sibling.

4. Children Not Doing as They are Told

Of all the things that frustrates parents most of all, it is this "crash" area. This is the one that drives parents berserk. This is the one that confuses parents most of all. This is the one that makes parents almost blow a fuse.

> - "Why can't they do it the first time I ask them?"
> - "Why does it have to take me asking them three times before they actually do it?"
> - "Sometimes I wonder if they are really deaf!"

- *"Why do I have to yell and scream before they go and do what I want?"*
- *"What's the matter with these kids that they won't do what they're asked?"*
- *"I end up threatening that they'll lose their TV or Game Boy before they actually go and do it!"*

Parents make simple requests like "Please come to the table for dinner" or "Please put your sneakers away" or "Please put your lunchbox on the sink" or "Please turn off the TV now" and so on. Generally, without fail, these requests do not get done; at least not on the first occasion that the parent makes the request. Certainly, they might get done on the third or fourth request or when the parent raises their voice or threatens a punishment of some sort, but these requests do not get done on the first ask.

So now we know what the major "crash" areas of the family might be.

Of course, in your household, there might be some other additions to these four major crash areas.

For example, your child might have a problem going to bed at night, or more exactly, staying in bed at night. In other words, once put to bed with the light out, some children find endless excuses to call out or get out of bed, which intrudes into the parents' own time at the end of the day when the parent is no doubt tired and exhausted.

I recall in my own household that one particular crash area was first thing in the morning when my three children would get into the car for me to drop them off at school. Each of the three wanted to sit in the front seat. Needless to say, there was always the argument about whose turn it was and without fail, it always ended up in an argument with one or two of the children as well as myself feeling badly. What a way to start the day! It left most of us in a bad mood. I never seemed to be able to win.

The Rules Wheel

No matter what call I made as to whose turn it might be, there were at least two other children who did not agree with my decision and who let me know about it in no uncertain terms. It was hardly an effective way to begin the day.

So, as I said, you may have your own personal "hot spot" which is specific to your family and your routine, but nevertheless, **the principle still holds that if we have a problem area, the first thing we have to do is set some clear rules around the issue.**

Step 3: Set the Rules Clearly

When we set the rules, it is absolutely critical that they be very clear and not at all vague.

As indicated above, vague rules are almost as bad as no rules at all. **The rules have to be clear.** How do we make them clear?

There are three important points to keep in mind when making the rules. They are as follows.

1. Make the Rules Very Specific with No Loopholes

Children are smart. We were smart when we were children. Children always seem to be looking for the loopholes. As parents, we need to understand this. We need to make the job easier for ourselves and not harder.

If we make a rule, we need to **make sure that it is tight** and that we have nailed it down with no loose ends. For example, rather than "Put your school bag away" it could be, "Please put your school bag in the hallway cupboard as soon as you come in the front door from school." We do not want the situation where we are arguing about the interpretation of the rules! The rules need to stand as they are and be **very clear and specific.**

2. Make the Rules Positively Worded

The rules have to be **positive**. We want to draw attention to those behaviors that we **want**, not draw attention to those behaviors that we don't want.

We need to focus on the positive and highlight the kinds of behaviors that we want to see more of rather than focus on those behaviors that we are trying to see less of and are trying to leave behind.

3. Put the Rules on a Poster

Remember that **children are very visual and not auditory**. The eyes work well, but the ears don't.

If you go into any First Grade or Kindergarten class you will be instantly reminded how children learn because it is a kaleidoscope of colors, shapes, patterns, designs and visual information.

Furthermore, children (like many adults) have selective listening and have selective memories and often we end up arguing about what we thought the other person said or meant to say.

Putting it on a poster eliminates all doubt about what was intended and what was meant. It is clear and it can be seen.

Finally, the poster needs to be placed in a public place for all to see. Just like a road sign. They are placed where they can be easily seen.

With posters, therefore, the most likely places might be on the fridge or on the pin board in the kitchen area or family room and additional copies might also be placed in the child's bedroom (e.g. on his wall, pin board or the back of his door).

I have certainly had some children who have been very proud of their posters while others have been somewhat sensitive or embarrassed that their friends or extended family

The Rules Wheel

might see the posters and naturally enquire what it is all about. In this instance, this needs to be negotiated with the children and a compromise reached. It may be, for example, that the poster on the back of their bedroom door remains while poster in the kitchen area is taken down.

Examples of Rules

Morning Routine

Given the above and the three step process that needs to occur in setting the rules, let's take the ***Morning Routine*** as a first example of how these steps can be implemented.

First, work out what the steps are that the child needs to undertake from the time she gets up in the morning to the time she walks out the door to go to school.

Of course, you can also ask your child to help work out the steps that everyone needs to go through in the morning routine.

Remember to be specific and positively word it. For the Morning Routine, it might look like this, as shown in the box below (although every household will be slightly different):

Morning Routine

- ➢ **Get Up**
- ➢ **Toilet**
- ➢ **Breakfast**
- ➢ **Get Dressed**
- ➢ **Make the Bed**
- ➢ **Do Hair / Teeth**
- ➢ **Pack Bag**
- ➢ **Leave the House**

Of course, it will depend on your family as to how specific or what detail you need to go to in each of these steps.

If breakfast, for example, is a time when children typically fight over the choice of breakfast food, then there will need to be some comment or direction which helps to alleviate this (e.g. a rotation system for who goes first or a specific breakfast food allocated for each child).

By the way, if you want particular jobs or tasks to be done such as making the bed, then they should be listed in the Routine.

Don't be like the two parents who sat in front of me with their 13 and 15-year-old teenagers and asked, "How can we get our two daughters to make their bed, keep their room tidy and help around the house"?

If you want to create good habits, you have to do so early in life.

It can be difficult sometimes to teach an old dog new tricks, as they say.

What you want to do is create good habits for your children. Creating good habits that will assist them in their daily life and make life easier for them to handle than otherwise might be the case.

Now, let me ask you a question. Is the Morning Routine that is listed above in the box tight enough? Have we covered the loopholes or loose-ends? Is it sufficient?

The answer is no.

If you wanted to leave the house at say, 8:15am, would it be okay for your child to finally get out of bed at 8:00am or 8:05am? Of course, the answer is "no way." So, the list might be in the right order, but there is still one big loophole ....namely, time.

In order to close that loophole, therefore, perhaps the rule and poster could look like that as outlined below.

Morning Routine

- Get up   7:10am
- Toilet   7:15 – 7:20am (5 minutes)
- Breakfast   7:20 – 7:35am (15 minutes)
- Get dressed   7:35 – 7:45am (10 minutes)
- Make the bed   7:45 – 7:50am (5 minutes)
- Do hair / teeth 7:50 – 7:55am (5 minutes)
- Pack bag   7:55 – 8:00am (5 minutes)

- Free time   8.00 – 8.15am (15 minutes)

- Leave the house   8.15am

What we work out in the first instance is what time we want to leave the house. Then we work backwards to establish what time the child needs to get up in the morning.

When you are first arranging this schedule, you can afford to be somewhat generous in the time allocated to do each task. In other words, if you think it only takes your child about 10 minutes to have breakfast, then allow 15 minutes in order to be sure that he will achieve what is required within the stipulated time.

As an aside, if your child is at an age where they cannot yet read a clock (either one with hands or one that is digital) then simply use the oven timer (or any timer) which usually has a bell or buzzer or alternatively, use a small hourglass. I have also had some parents who instructed children about the minute hand on the clock and said something like "okay, now you need to finish your breakfast by the time the big hand has moved on to the seven."

In relation to time, is also important to mention that the minutes column on the far right-hand side for the Morning Routine shown above is the most important column rather than the center column outlining the exact time periods according to the clock.

In other words, if your child decided to get up at 6am and then do all of his or her tasks within the allocated time periods (i.e. 5, 10 or 15 minutes), then you would be very pleased with that as a parent (and no doubt so would they), and of course, you would not be at all concerned that your child had not stuck to the exact clock schedules.

If too, your child wants to get up earlier in order to have more free time at the end, then that should be encouraged as well. It's win-win. Your child is ready so you can leave at the stipulated time, but more particularly, your child has had more free time or playtime. Both of you are happy.

You will also notice that I have also inserted **a period of "free time"** into the Morning Routine. In a sense, **this serves two purposes**.

First, it is a reward time for the child to watch television, read, play games, play on the computer or do whatever they wish. With all their tasks done, it is now time for play. What is the principle that I'm trying to teach? Work first, then play. It is a good habit for life.

Second, this free time is a buffer zone. If anything comes unstuck (as it usually does in the morning), then you have this buffer zone which helps to ensure that you still get out of the door on time.

Because children are visual, **the poster** needs to be appealing and needs to be dressed up. For example, some of the parents that I talk to have made up fairly bright and interesting posters on their computers.

It may be only A4 size or US Letter size, but it uses bright colors and uses Clipart computer programs, for example, in order to make it more attractive. Other parents have made up posters where they have cut out pictures from magazines to illustrate each step.

For instance, from a toothpaste advertisement, they have cut out pictures of toothbrushes and toothpaste or found pictures of breakfast cereal. In this regard, the sky is the limit. Be imaginative. Be creative.

Importantly, get your children involved in making the poster so that it becomes their work too and they start to own it. It becomes an enjoyable parent-child activity that you can both work on together.

Evening Routine

Now using the Morning Routine as a guide, you can pull together the *Evening Routine*.

Even though it might be called the Evening Routine, it actually starts from the moment that the child comes home from school and walks in that front door (it is really the Afternoon/Evening rule, but I have found it easier just to call it the Evening Routine).

Depending on your home situation though, the Evening Rule might look something like the following on the next page.

Evening Routine

- Home from school — 4:00pm
- Put lunch box on kitchen sink — 4:00 – 4:05pm (5 minutes)
- Put school notes on table — 4:00 – 4:05pm (5 minutes)
- Put bag away — 4:00 – 4:05pm (5 minutes)
- Change out of uniform — 4:10 – 4:20pm (10 minutes)
- Afternoon tea — 4:20 – 4:50pm (30 minutes)
- Homework — 4:50 – 5:35pm (45 minutes)
- Free Time — 5:35 – 6:00pm (25 minutes)
- Set the table — 6:00 – 6:05pm (5 minutes)
- Tea — 6:05 – 6:35pm (30 minutes)
- Help with the dishes — 6:35 – 6:50pm (15 minutes)
- Homework — 6:50 – 7:30pm (40 minutes)
- Television — 7:30 – 8:00pm (30 minutes)
- Bath / shower — 8:00 – 8:15pm (15 minutes)
- Teeth / Toilet — 8:15 – 8:20pm (5 minutes)
- Read stories — 8:20 – 8:35pm (15 minutes)
- Bed time (lights out) — 8:35pm

As has been said before, every household is different, but nevertheless, the rules need to be tight, with no loopholes, and positively worded.

*Of course, this does **not** mean that you run the household like an army camp.*

In the afternoon and evening for example, there are often alterations to the routine due to things like sports practice, music lessons, extra tuition, extra curricular activities like debating, chess or the science club to name a few. Some parents have two sets of Evening / Afternoon routines one of which might be a Monday, Wednesday and Friday routine whereas the other one might be a Tuesday and Thursday routine when the child has after-school activities.

In some cases too, the Evening Routine may not start until around 6pm when the child is collected from after school care, the grandparents' house or the house of a family friend. In this kind of situation though, there ought to be an expectation that the child does undertake some homework even though the parent may not be there to supervise such efforts.

Nevertheless, a quiet word to the director of the after school care center about your expectations for homework can often mean that the homework is supervised. Otherwise, many parents would complain that once they leave work and pick up their child from after school care, they are straight into meal preparation and there seems to be little time for homework, let alone the other activities that tend to fill the night before the child goes to bed.

Where there are two or more children in the family, the Evening Routine can often be the same for each child. Occasionally, there can be slight variations for one child versus the other particularly for things such as getting ready for bed where one child might be in the shower or the bathroom and the other child might be having story-time with a parent.

Again, this Evening Routine needs to be put on a **poster** for all to see. Make it appealing and attractive and invite your child to help you put it together.

Children Fighting and Not Getting On

Where there is more than one child, fighting seems to be a frequent problem.

Somehow or other children do not seem to get along. They find endless ways to taunt each other and tease. They manage to find all sorts of little and devious ways to annoy each other, which may include things like making faces, and making noises as well as saying particular things and doing particular things that they know will get a response.

Although the principles for rule-setting are to make it very specific and positively worded, how you actually set up this rule really does depend on the kinds of behaviors you see your children doing that annoy or infuriate the other child.

For example, if you are aware of name calling and "putdowns," then your rule ought to be directed specifically at this behavior.

If you were aware of hitting, pushing and so forth, then your rule ought to be directed specifically at this kind of behavior. See the kinds of examples below.

> **When you talk to each other, use pleasant words, talk nicely and encourage each other.**

> **When you are around each other, you keep your hands, feet and other body parts to yourself.**

Children Doing as They are Told

Let's look at another rule. Of all the rules that might be put in place within the family, **this is probably the most important one**. It underpins all sorts of other rules. In a sense, it is the foundation rule.

Let me ask you this question: *When you ask your children to do something, what do you want?*

Now, I have asked this question thousands of times. Almost without fail, either within my consulting office or at the parenting seminars that I have run, the answer will usually come back that parents just want their children to *"do it."*

Typically, following that kind of response (which is essentially true), I often play the devil's advocate and ask:

- Is that all that you really want as parents?
- Would it be okay for me to "do it," but do so being grumpy and negative?

All parents will reply no, that it's not okay to be grumpy and that they want me to be pleasant when I "do it." So I tell them that if there are no loopholes, then that has to be included in the rule was well. As well as me "doing it," I now have to do it pleasantly and nicely.

Playing the devil's advocate a bit further, I then ask parents:

- Would it be okay for me to "do it" and be pleasant about it, but do it in my own time?
- Could I do it when I wanted to, such as when I had finished playing or when I had finished watching my television show or at the next commercial break on the television?

Of course, the answer is again no. Parents want me to do it now, straight away. This therefore, has to be in the rule too.

So what does the rule really look like when we have been specific, with no loopholes, and we have worded the rule positively, bringing attention to the kind of behaviors that we want rather than the behaviors that we don't want?

The rule would look something like the following:.

> **What do you do when Mom and Dad ask you to do something?**
>
> 1. **Be polite and say "Yes"**
>
> 2. **Start now**
>
> 3. **Do it quickly**

This kind of rule would tend to give you as a parent what you wanted from your child when you asked him or her to do something. Naturally, if you did ask your child to do something and she was nice and started straight away and did it quickly, then is probably safe to say that you would almost drop dead!

Reality shows me that generally speaking, most children will follow this rule about 50% of the time. Occasionally, it may reach even 70%.

If the child responded in this way 90% of the time, there would be something dreadfully wrong!

I can also tell you that if your child is only following this rule about 10% of the time, then your home life is probably going to be chaotic, there is probably a good deal of yelling and screaming, you are probably at your wit's end and wondering how you can sell your child!

The Rules Wheel

Now that you have set your rules, how do you implement them? How you get them to actually work for you?

More particularly, how do you combine **both** the **wheel of love** and the **wheel of rules** to come together into a practical "see and do" program that can assist both you and your children?

This is discussed in the following chapter.

CHAPTER 4 SUMMARY

The other important wheel on the journey of parenting is how to set rules and boundaries.

Given that we surround our children with unconditional love that is designed to enhance their self-esteem and we explore their talents in order to give them self-confidence, the task now is to set boundaries in which they can live and move and in which they can keep themselves safe and secure.

Step 1: Set the Rules

Generally speaking, there are two major problems in families when it comes to rules or setting boundaries.

Firstly, often there are none. Secondly, if there are any rules, then typically they are vague.

Step 2: Set the Right Rules

Which rules do we set? How do we know which rules we should put in place? How do we work out which rules to have?

Simply work out where you have most arguments and most conflict and see what rule you can put in place as an important first step in bringing some order and some harmony back into the family.

My own clinical observation shows that that there are basically *four* major "crash" areas in almost every family.

Of course, it can vary somewhat between families, but overall, there is an overwhelming consensus that says without

The Rules Wheel

fail, most families have "crashes" at four particular "intersections."

What are those four areas?

1. **Morning Routine**
2. **Evening Routine**
3. **Children Fighting or Not Getting On**
4. **Children Not Doing as They are Told**

Step 3: Set the Rules Clearly

When we set the rules, it is absolutely critical that they must be very clear and not at all vague. How do we make them clear?

There are three important points to keep in mind when making the rules. They are as follows.

1. **Make the Rules Very Specific with No Loopholes**
2. **Make the Rules Positively Worded**
3. **Put the Rules on a Poster**

Examples of Rules

How to make the rules really work for you.

CHAPTER 5

MAKING IT ALL WORK

To this point, we have discussed how critical it is that the child is loved unconditionally which then provides the backdrop for allowing the next wheel of parenting to be included, namely, the rules and boundaries.

How these two both work together is discussed below.

It's critical to remember though, that **both are important**. Both wheels allow the bike to move forward and the journey to happen.

Remember in Chapter 2 (*The Two Wheels of Parenting*) how problems arose for children (and their parents) when one wheel was dysfunctional or worse still, when both wheels ceased to function?

At all times, both wheels need to be in good order for the journey to move forward. And of course, it is assumed that the parent is providing the role model about how to ride the bike and how to make it all happen.

Setting up the Program

In the first instance, it is assumed that the parent or parents have given sufficient thought to how they can demonstrate unconditional love and at the same time consider what rules would assist the family to function better. It is assumed, as has been indicated above, that the parent is setting the role model for how to communicate and how to interact and that this program is simply an extension of how family members can relate and communicate.

Family Conference

Once the parent has done their own home work, one way of ensuring that all the members of the family are involved is to organize what is called a *family conference.*

Of course, communications among family members is meant to happen informally and naturally, but the nature of this program is to include everyone and make sure that everyone helps in formulating the plan about how the family can work together better.

What happens at this particular family conference? Families take the opportunity to talk about how things are running generally. (Now it is assumed that things are not running well or could, in fact, run better because this is why the parent is keen on implementing a practical "see and do" program.)

The parent could ask, "How well are the family routines working"? "Are we feeling good about the morning routine and getting off to school"? "Could it run better"? "In what way"? "Are there any grievances or gripes to be aired"? "What could the family do more of"? "What could the family do less of"?

The family members take it in turn to give comment and the family moves systematically around the group giving their viewpoints. Ultimately, the parent will need to provide input about the kinds of routines that need to be put in place in the kinds of rules which would help the family function better.

Indeed, on occasion, the children might comment that they would be happy to follow the rules and regulations if the parent did not yell or scream so much.

Certainly, children generally respond positively to the notion of rules being implemented, simply because some children enjoy the structure and order while others enjoy the fact that there are rewards to be gained for following the program and helping it to function.

The Ingredients

Once the new schedule has been discussed and the need for it outlined at a family conference, there is a period of time (i.e. perhaps a week or more) when necessary preparations are made before the program actually begins.

In other words, the rules need to be put onto the **posters**. The children generally like to help in this regard either by designing it on their computer or cutting out pictures from magazines and papers. Remember, this is their program too and now they need to start to own it and take responsibility for it.

The poster needs to be devised outlining the **rewards** that children receive by keeping to the program (this is discussed below in more detail).

Finally, the parent needs to organize **"tokens"** which are given out and which help both the parent and child to stay on task (see below for further comment on these too).

The Program Begins

The family decides when and on what day the program will commence. Everyone is agreed that on a certain day, the new schedule will begin.

> "Before I got married, I had six theories about bringing up children; now I have six children and no theories."
>
> (John Wilmot; 1647-1680, Earl of Rochester)

Step 1: Immediately Give Out Consequences

Remember how I indicated previously that children are concrete, literal thinkers who only really know about "now" time? That is to say, telling a small child that he or she will get a reward at the end of the day or at the end of the week is like telling an adult that they will receive a bonus in 10 years' time.

Children have little conception about how far in the future a week might be, or a month, or anything else for that matter. In the same way, they have little idea of what it might mean to talk about time past. What's most important to them is now.

If you really want to make an impact on a child's behavior (and this goes for adults as well, for that matter), then any consequence (positive or negative) has to be given out immediately. In other words, as soon as the behavior occurs (either good or bad) a consequence has to immediately follow (again, either positive or negative).

Somehow or other, we forget this basic principle of human nature. Let me say it again. *Once a behavior occurs, the consequence, either positive or negative, has to occur **immediately after** you see or hear the particular behavior.* The child then locks in the consequence with the behavior. All of a sudden, the behavior has meaning because it is associated with a consequence.

I have lost count of the number of parents who might be well-intentioned, but who say things to their children like, "If you are good all day, I will give you a [...special treat...] tonight."

Not only is there a problem with the term "good" being so vague and wishy-washy, but more particularly, at the end of the day, the child will not be able to remember anything about the day, let alone whether they were good or bad!

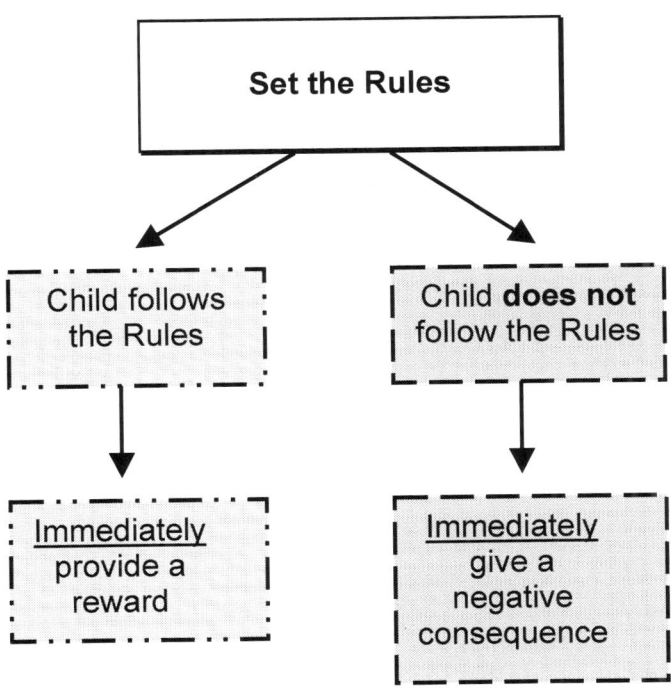

Getting a reward like a fudge or candy at the end of the day will mean more to the adult than it will for the child! Remember that children are concrete, literal thinkers. Their brain has not developed sufficiently to understand the concept of time. There is only one time for children and it is called "now" time. So, if for children there is only "now" time, then rewards and punishments have to be given out "now."

Worse still, I have also had well-intentioned parents who have said to their children, for example, that if they were good for the week (not just for one day), they would get a special treat on Friday night. Friday night for some children is an eternity away! Again, this time sequence might mean something for the adult, but it means nothing for the child.

If as a parent you're trying to train a behavior such as being "good," then there is absolutely no way that you will be successful using a reward at the end of the week. It is just too far away. The child has to be reinforced now.

Alternatively, for negative behavior, the child has to be given a negative consequence now. There is no other way.

Remember too that children's ears do not work as well as their eyes, so giving a verbal consequence (especially yelling) is not as powerful as a visual and "action" consequence.

I will explain this in more detail below.

"The first half of our lives is ruined by our parents, and the second half by our children."

(Clarence Darrow
American Lawyer, 1857-1938)

Step 2: Reward for Following the Rules

If you want a behavior to reoccur, then **the moment that you see it, reinforce it with a positive consequence**.

Your child does as he or she is told – or perhaps the child does something on their own accord without being asked

As a parent, you immediately say something positive –
"Thanks Jason, I really like the way that you came to the table for dinner as soon as you were called....that's great."

You may also use a pat on the head or the shoulder or some other form of physical touch

You straight away give out a "token" – something that the child can see and feel

What do I mean by reinforce? How do you reinforce a positive behavior or a behavior that you want to see more of?

I know this sounds like a very basic question, but somehow or other, when it comes to parenting, some parents seem to lose their common sense.

1. Use Verbal Praise

In my clinical practice, I am no longer surprised when people say to me that they don't remember how their parents praised them – or, in fact, if their parents ever did praise them. Often, the only praise they can recall was indirect, such as hearing their parents talking to other people outside the family, but within earshot of them.

Interestingly, though, people tend to have little difficulty remembering how their parents criticized them. How is it in your family?

Sitting in a waiting room some years back, I idly picked up a magazine, flicked through it and came across an article titled, "The Power of Praise."

It started me thinking, especially in relation to parents and parenting practices. Let me ask you, when did you last encourage and praise your children?

> **Praise is powerful and is a major factor in giving children a healthy self-esteem -- so it is staggering how rarely parents use it.**

Often, we are often regarded as a community of "knockers." Indeed, such is also frequently the case in the family setting. As parents, we are very adept at catching our

Making it all Work

children out; we find it very easy to catch them being bad and are quick to pull them up and criticize.

As a consequence, much of our communication with our children is negative and judgmental.

> *We need to remember that **being encouraging and appreciative of others and what they do is critical to their developing self-confidence, self-esteem and the ability to cope**.*
>
> This is a **key** for parents.

One of the most commonly asked questions by parents is, "What can I do to give my children self-confidence"? The answer is relatively simple. It has to do with **praise**. Encouragement. Giving positive feedback. Remembering to say that you love them. It's really quite simple, but somehow or other, we don't do it as parents.

Remember the wheel of love. Sitting as a basic wheel to this program is unconditional love.

Of course, giving praise for what your child has done is conditional. Both, therefore, have a role to play i.e. unconditional and conditional. In a sense it is the unconditional love that supports and nurtures the child's self-esteem while the other hand, it is the conditional praise that nurtures the child's self-confidence.

What would happen if we made a concerted effort to praise and encourage? And I'm not talking about the times when our son or daughter comes home with an 'A' grade for the math or spelling test, or when he tops the batting average for the season, or when she is top goalie. They are the easy times to praise.

I'm really talking about the little, nitty-gritty everyday things that continually occur in families;
- like praise for coming to the table for dinner when you first called;
- like thanking them for taking their cup out to the kitchen sink;
- like saying you appreciate them saying "excuse me" when they want to interrupt your conversation;
- like telling them that you really like it when you see them sit and read;
- like saying how much you appreciate it when they sat in the car together without bickering;
- like saying how you like it when they talk to you.

It's absolutely fascinating how many parents have difficulty praising and appreciating their children. It sounds so straight forward, but it happens all too rarely.

Parents often consider, for example, that "kids should know how to behave anyway," that "they shouldn't get thanks all the time," that "they shouldn't expect to get rewards," and that "they might get a big head." Hang on a minute. Who's got the problem here? Hint: it's not the children.

People like to be appreciated – big people and little people – and both flourish with appropriate and even generous doses of praise and positive feedback.

If you're wondering why all your talking and criticism isn't working, try a little positive talk. As I once read on my desk calendar, "the place for a knocker is outside the door." There's certainly no place for such in the home or in the family.

Making it all Work

Instead of being intent on catching your children being bad, try it the other way round. **Catch them being good and you might just get some pleasant surprises.**

2. Use a Physical Touch or Gesture

As well as verbal praise, which **always** has to be used, it is sometimes appropriate to use a physical gesture or touch as a way of reinforcing the behavior.

Sometimes a pat on the head or the shoulder can have a very profound effect. Sometimes an open show of affection such as a kiss or a hug can be a very powerful reinforcer.

Of course, both physical touch or the display of affection need to be genuine on the part of the parent. This is not playing at reinforcement. Often when the parent is delighted or pleased in the way that their child has responded, it is only natural that there is a physical touch or some affection towards the child.

3. Hand out a Token

Remember that children are visual and not auditory.

Remember too that in their early years, they are very much about touching and doing.

As a result, as soon as the child behaves appropriately (i.e. he or she gets out of bed at the right time, or eats their breakfast within the specified time, and does as a parent asks), the parent not only gives verbal praise, but importantly, hands out what is called a "token."

What is a "token"?

It is something physical that they get in their hand. They see it. They can touch it and feel it.

For example, it might be a paddle pop stick or a colored piece of cardboard created by the parent and the child. I have had a dentist who told me that he cut the plastic tops off of amalgams.

Examples of Tokens

- ✓ Paddle pop sticks
- ✓ Macaroni
- ✓ Washers
- ✓ Clothes buttons
- ✓ Golf tees
- ✓ Toy buttons
- ✓ Pieces of cardboard
- ✓ Pieces of metal

I have had parents who have gone off to toy stores and bought colored buttons similar to what some parents will remember as a child was called "tiddlywinks." I have had a car mechanic and a plumber who used nuts or screw washers to hand out to their children.

Importantly, any tokens that are used need to be counterfeit proof. In other words, if you have two or more children and you're using buttons, then each child ought to have a different colored button. This also stops any black-market trading that might go on!

With my plumber and car mechanic, they both stamped the initial of the particular child's first name on the washers. With the parent who used little squares of colored cardboard, each piece of cardboard had the parent's signature or initials on it.

Remember that children are smart, and we were too, so the program has to be foolproof.

Having said that, I still remember the mother who came into my office telling me about her 10-year-old daughter. Over the years, the mother had previously collected a tin of clothes buttons from shirts, pants, coats and the like and she decided to use these as tokens. She was initially very impressed that her daughter had earned a good number of buttons until she went to her daughter's wardrobe one day and realized that every garment had been stripped of its buttons!

Of course, receiving praise as well as receiving a token can be a powerful reinforcement since both are received immediately after the behavior occurs, but more particularly, *it is what the tokens represent that is more powerful*.

Having said that, the "tokens" **should not** be money. Using money only defeats the purpose of the program since money in and off itself has other major connotations about how we live and survive.

I have seen that when parents use money as the immediate reward for their children, the children get to a point where they won't do anything unless they are paid ("How much are you gonna give me?" "What's it worth to clean your car?" "Give me 10 bucks and I'll mow the lawn for you."). Such, unfortunately, is the power of money.

Instead, the "token," because it is not associated with the community's values or our culture, is an innocuous kind of reinforcement.

It is just important that it can be seen and felt by children; remember that children are "see and do."

4. The Tokens are Traded In

Of course, once the children have the tokens in hand, which it is true to say are reinforcers in themselves, then it is important that they have the opportunity to trade their tokens in on treats and rewards.

This is really the fun bit for children. They have helped the family run, and they have received their rewards. They are often proud of their collection of tokens.

In a sense, this is what you actually do with your salary. You gain "tokens" called money or a pay-packet and then you trade these in for goods and services e.g. food, clothes, household effects, and then you save some for entertainment, holidays, luxury goods and so on. This is how it works for children as well. There really is no difference. What is good for the adults is good for the children.

These reward lists need to be individualized for each child. What one child sees as a reward is not what another child will necessarily see as a reward.

I remember one little boy who would do anything for spaghetti bolognaise. Another loved to trade in his tokens for 20 minutes with his father kicking the football in the park. Another would save vehemently to rent computer games from the local store. Another traded in his tokens to gradually buy and collect a special set of hero cards.

One little girl saved to get a special doll that she wanted while another had her eye on an alarm clock that was quite unique. Another girl used her tokens to go and stay extra time at her Nana's house. The children need to say what it is that they would like to receive as treats.

Possible Treats

- Favorite meal or special drink
- Sweets, favorite fruit / muesli bar, juice
- Activities like watching TV, going on the computer, playing in the park
- Special treats like going to the movies, hiring a DVD, getting take-away to eat, sleepovers

Of course, such treats should not break the bank in terms of what the children receive. These "treats" need to be the kinds of things that the children receive as part of their daily routines. The treats should **not** be excessive nor outlandish.

Step 3: Negative Consequences for Not Following the Rules

Of course, your children will not always follow the rules. You already know this. So, what do we do? Well, I can tell you that most parents confess to "ranting and raving," threatening all sorts of punishments and at times, wanting to spank or "strangle" their children.

Instead, **we need a strategy that is planned and thought out**. This is no time to be flying by the seat of your pants, as the saying goes. This is no time to be thinking on your feet because if you do as a parent, you will come unstuck, louse it up and then feel angry or guilty (or both) afterwards.

Therefore, you may like to try the following.

1. Ignore the Poor Behavior of one Child and Reward the Behavior of the Other

If you have two or more children and you ask them to do something like "come to the table for dinner" and one does and the other doesn't, usually what we do as parents is get angry or annoyed with the one who hasn't come.

Try another approach.

Instead, ignore the fact that your other child has not come to the table and reward the one who has come. The result can be quite startling.

Rewarding the child who has come to the table keeps the situation positive instead of you as the parent calling out to the disobedient child and saying things like, "How many times do I have to tell you to come to the table"? The child who has come to the table is rewarded and feels good and this also makes a powerful statement to the other child who hasn't come to the table, because their sibling has been rewarded with a token.

If you only have one child in your family then of course this is difficult to do. With two or more children, however, this kind of technique can be used very powerfully and as indicated, it really does keep the whole home situation positive rather than entering the domain of bad feelings and people feeling disgruntled.

2. Rewind or Rehearse the Correct Behavior

This is a fairly traditional technique, but somehow or other, parents have forgotten to use it.

When one child, for example, does a behavior that you do not like or want such as running through the kitchen, then you say "stop," and get her to go back and walk through the kitchen appropriately.

Remember that children learn more through "see and do" than by you lecturing them. Getting them to actually "do" the behavior that you want is more powerful than you talking or haranguing them.

Of course, this needs to happen *every* time that the child runs through the kitchen. Consistency is very important in parenting.

It becomes more etched into their brain because they actually go through the motions themselves rather than you just telling them about it.

3. Apply Natural Consequences

On occasion, if the child creates a problem, then it can be "fixed" by undertaking a logical consequence. For example, if the child happens to spill his milk, then it should be a matter of

Making it all Work 101

asking the child to rectify the damage and to clean up the mess or spill.

Remember, this is not a time to rant and rave and say things like, "you're always so clumsy" or "you always spill things." Such comments are destructive and eat away at self-esteem and create in the children's mind a negative picture of themselves.

4. Loss of Privileges

If the child continues to push limits and not do as he or she is told, then taking away particular privileges is certainly appropriate.

For example, as a parent, you may take away television or the use of the computer for the afternoon, or the use of the computer or you could indicate to your child that she will not be going over to the neighbor's house to play or that she has lost the use of the PlayStation for the rest of the day.

What is really important in this instance is that the loss of privileges occurs close to the misdemeanor or offending behavior.

In other words, if your child continues to push limits then it is not appropriate to say something like, "That's it, you've lost television for the next week."

After about the second night of no television, everyone seems to forget what on earth this was all about and frequently goes back to television watching.

What does this say to the child? It says that punishment is no big deal because the parent will forget about it anyway and secondly, it loses its overall desired effect because the action of the negative consequence is too far removed from the actual misdemeanor or poor behavior.

> **What is absolutely critical is that the loss of privileges has to occur *close* to the misdemeanor or poor behavior.**

Remember again that children are concrete, literal thinkers who really only seem to know about "now" time. If your child continues to create trouble, take away the privilege, but make sure that this happens soon after the inappropriate behavior.

5. Sitting Out from an Activity

Sitting out from a game or activity is a kind of mini time-out. The research shows quite clearly that time-out is the most effective means of teaching children. They do not like to be removed from the activity or to be separated from what is going on.

> **Research shows that Time-Out is the most effective means of teaching children.**

Sitting out from an activity could be as simple as one child sitting under the carport for five minutes while the other child sits under the pergola.

In other words, if one minute your children are playing nicely in the backyard and the next minute they are fighting or pushing and shoving, then separating them to different parts of the yard is a very effective intervention.

… This is a "see and do" intervention which does not mean that you have to raise your voice or launch into a lecture on sharing or playing nicely or whatever. Instead, you simply allocate places where each child needs to be for the next five minutes.

"What if they won't go," I hear you say. We will cover this in point No. 6, because it is important that children understand that you are in charge and even though they might like to, they do not yet have the wisdom and maturity to be able to run the family.

"What if they don't stay there for the full five minutes?" you might ask. You simply start the time over again.

Remember, you are in charge and although your children may like to push limits and see if there are any loopholes such as getting away with less than the five minutes, it is important for them to understand that five minutes is five minutes and that you are a person of your word who follows through.

6. Time-out

Let me repeat that timeout is the most effective means of teaching children about inappropriate or poor behavior.

Time-out ought to be mandatory for any aggressive or violent behavior. This includes swearing, mouthing off, shouting abuse, calling names, angry outbursts or any other form of verbal aggressiveness.

This also includes, of course, any physical actions such as hitting, kicking, pinching, pulling, biting, breaking things, destroying things or any other form of aggressive behavior. This kind of behavior cannot be tolerated.

As a psychologist, I note that we seem to becoming more aggressive and violent in our community as evidenced by things such as "road rage" and "supermarket line rage" to just mention two, as well as the fact that in work environments there also seems to be an increase in bullying, harassment and conflict certainly since the early 1990's.

What do you use for time-out? Is the bedroom okay? If possible, try not to use the bedroom. The bedroom is for sleeping and generally, bedrooms are fun places to be where children have their toys, books and belongings. Time-out is supposed to be just that, time-out. The bedroom therefore, does not always fulfill that requirement. Sometimes too, if a bedroom is shared between siblings, then the bedroom is not a good solution because it unnecessarily penalizes the other sibling who can't get access to the room while time-out is in process.

However, some parents certainly have used the bedroom with the instruction for the child to simply sit on the bed. This seems to work well providing it is clear that the child sits on the bed and does not play with all the toys.

Alternatively, look around your house for a relatively boring room or place. This might be the laundry room or the bathroom or perhaps a spare room. It might be a place like a chair under the stairwell or a chair at the end of the corridor by the front door. Nevertheless, *it has to be away from family activity.*

If, for example, you did use a laundry room or bathroom, then you would need to ensure that it was safe to do so, and any ingredients, chemicals, appliances or whatever would need to be safely stored and locked away. Even something like extra rolls of toilet paper may have to be removed because I have certainly known some enterprising children who have tried to see how many rolls might fit down the cistern!

It is true that time-out can be anywhere. This is especially so whenever the family is away from the home.

For instance, at a picnic, time-out can be sitting by a tree or sitting back in the car. At a shopping centre, time-out can be sitting on a bench (e.g. "We're going to sit on the bench for five minutes while you calm down"). At a friend's or relative's house, time-out might mean sitting in a corner of the family room. The focus is on being removed from the activity and restoring appropriate behavior before returning to it.

A real strength of time-out is simply that: it is time away.

During this time children need to understand that time-out is a chance to calm down. It is a time and place for them to understand their feelings. It is a time and place for them to consider their options and think about making better choices.

Needless to say, it is also a good opportunity for the parent to have "time out." It is an opportunity for the parent to calm down, to get things in perspective and to reassess the situation; to see, for example, if perhaps the child might simply be overtired or whether the child could be excessively distressed, or perhaps over-excited for some reason.

Time-out is an advantage for both children and parents.

"What if they are making a noise or creating havoc during time-out?" is a question that is sometimes asked. Let them alone. This is their time-out.

However, if they are still making a noise at the end of the five minutes, it would not be appropriate to call an end to the time-out until they are quiet. Once they are quiet again, time-out can end and they can resume whatever they were doing.

If, however, they made a mess of the room and threw toys around, for example, then the principle of natural consequences ought to apply where they clean up before coming out of time-out.

"What if they won't go to time-out?" I am often asked. For little children (say, 5 - 7 year olds), who you can still pick up, carry or physically take them to the time-out room or area.

If you do this one or two times and the child understands that you are serious and you will follow through, then in my experience, you generally will not have to continue to physically place them in time-out and they will start to go by themselves.

For older children who are just simply too big to physically restrain or take to time-out, then consider using the following procedure:

Making it all Work

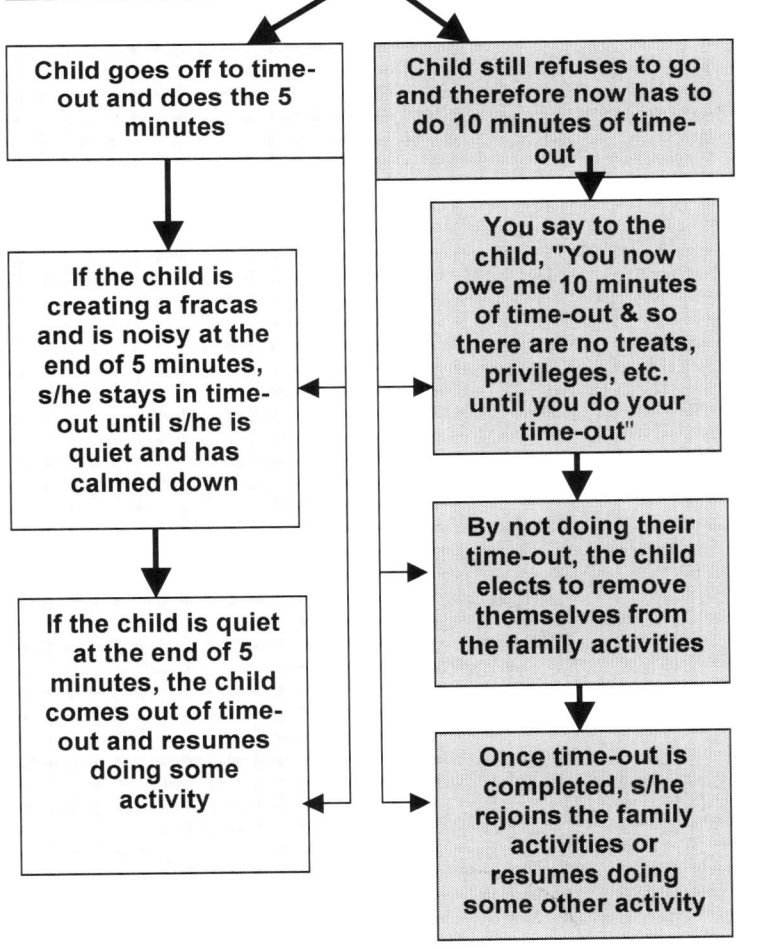

Again, it is important that the child understands who is in charge. As a parent, you do not have to be a dictator which is inappropriate, but you do need to be in charge.

7. Breaking the "Compliance" Rule

If you only needed to have one rule in the family, it would be the compliance rule.

That's the rule that asks, "What do you do when Mom and Dad ask you to do something?" This one rule underpins all of your requests and instructions to your child.

Because it is such an important rule and is the number one complaint from parents about what children don't do ("Why don't they just do as they are told?" "Why do I have to ask over and over?" "Why don't they just do it the first time I ask?"), then there is a special procedure for what to do if this rule is broken. This is shown over the next two pages.

You make a request of your child (e.g. *"Can you please come to the table for tea now?"*). The child is non-compliant i.e. he or she does not do one, two or all three of the following:
  1. Be polite and say yes
  2. Start now
  3. Do it quickly

You immediately say, *"Stop, what is the rule when Mum or Dad asks you to do something?"*
(Do not get into a big lecture, start to raise your voice or nag; instead, just follow the steps below)

Making it all Work

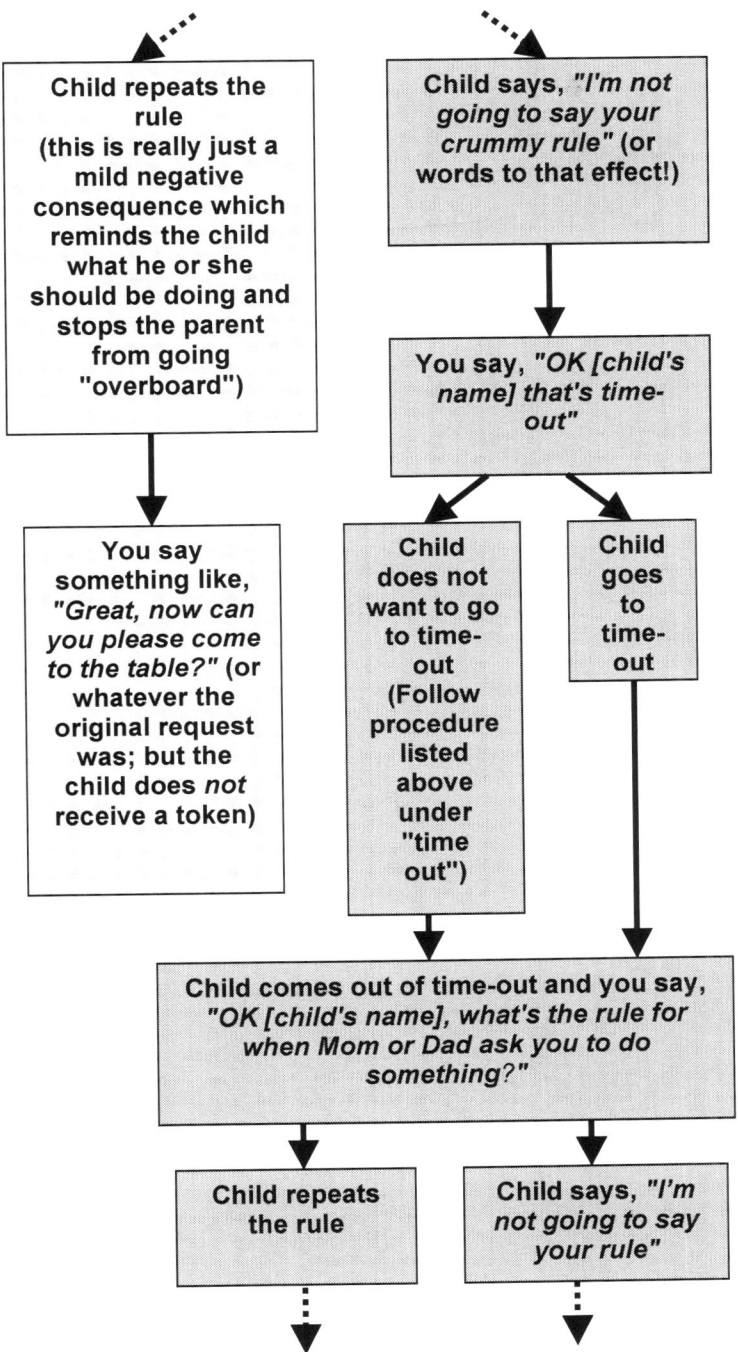

You say, "Good, now can you please sit at the table" (or whatever the original request was); and *don't* add any last liners like *"So next time, do it the first time I ask"* or *"That wasn't too hard now was it?"*	You say, "OK [child's name], that's time-out"; Send him or her back to time-out until child finally realizes that there are no loopholes and that they will need to say the rule

This procedure works well in that it gives parents a plan whereby they can handle children who do not follow requests or instructions.

Most parents do not have a plan about what to say or do if their children refuse to do as they are asked. Typically, the parents become frustrated and then angry and of course, they often say things and do things that they later regret.

In my experience, this procedure for coping with children who do not follow requests only breaks down if the parents do not control their own annoyance or anger.

Of course, you can expect that children will push the limits and try to find the loopholes. That's what children do and that's what we did as children. However, if parents consistently follow the procedure and hold their own emotions in check, the child will comply, realizing that there is no way out and no loopholes to be found.

You can expect at times that your child may well push this procedure perhaps for 20 or 30 minutes as a way of seeing who will give in first. In my experience though, a child will only ever do this once or at the most twice.

Children are smart. They recognize quickly whether or not there is anything to be gained from pursuing a particular action. If they see that there are no loopholes and that what they are doing is really not much fun, then typically they will decide to comply and assist.

Review Time

Once the program has been in place for around two weeks, it is entirely appropriate that there is a further family conference to review how it is progressing.

At that stage, it may need some tweaking or changing.

Conclusion

Let's reiterate.

There are two wheels of parenting, one called Love and one called Rules.

Neither of these particular wheels work well by themselves.

Irrespective, if you haven't seen change in 10 days with this program, there is something that has been omitted or left out. This program works.

"If you want to be something different, you have to do something different."

(Author unknown)

What is stopping you from trying it out? What have you got to lose?

More particularly, how would your family be if it did work? How would you feel if you knew your parenting was effective and you knew your children were happier and more content?

You owe it to yourself to try it out – if it doesn't work, then drop it. If it does work, how wonderful that might be.

"If you do what you've always done, you'll get what you've always got."

(Author unknown)

CHAPTER 5 SUMMARY

Start Out With the End in Mind

In the first instance, it is assumed that the parent or parents have given sufficient thought to how they can demonstrate unconditional love and at the same time consider what rules would assist the family to function better.

It is also assumed that the parent is setting the role model for how to communicate and how to interact and that this program is simply an extension of how family members can relate and communicate.

Family Conference

Once the parent has done their own home work, one way of ensuring that all the members of the family are involved is to organize what is called a *family conference.*

The Ingredients

Once the new schedule has been discussed and the need for it outlined at a family conference, there is a period of time (i.e. perhaps a week or more) when necessary preparations are made before the program actually begins.

The Program Begins

The family decides when and on what day the program will commence. Everyone is agreed that on a certain day, the new schedule will begin.

Step 1: Immediately Give Out Consequences

If you really want to make an impact on a child's behavior (and this goes for adults as well, for that matter), then any consequence (positive or negative) has to be given out immediately.

Step 2: Reward for Following the Rules

If you want a behavior to reoccur, then the moment you see it, reinforce it with a positive consequence.

1. Use Verbal Praise

Encouragement. Giving positive feedback. Remembering to say that you love them. It's really quite simple, but somehow or other, we don't do it as parents.

2. Use a Physical Touch or Gesture

It is sometimes appropriate to use a physical gesture or touch as a way of reinforcing the behavior. For example, a pat on the head or the shoulder can have a very profound effect.

3. Hand out a Token

Remember that children are visual and not auditory. As a result, as soon as the child behaves appropriately (i.e. he or she gets out of bed at the right time, or eats breakfast within the specified time, and does as a parent asks), the parent not only gives verbal praise, but importantly, hands out what is called a "token."

4. The Tokens are Traded In

Of course, once the children have the tokens in hand, which it is true to say are reinforcers in themselves, then it is important that they have the opportunity to trade their tokens in on various treats and rewards.

Step 3: Negative Consequences for Not Following the Rules

Of course, your children will not always follow the rules. Therefore, parents need a strategy that is planned and thought out.

This is no time to be thinking on your feet because if you do as a parent, you will come unstuck, louse it up and then feel angry or guilty (or both) afterwards.

Making it all Work

1. Ignore the Poor Behavior of one Child and Reward the Behavior of the Other

2. Rewind or Rehearse the Correct Behavior

3. Apply Natural Consequences

On occasion, if the child creates a problem, then it can be "fixed" by undertaking a logical consequence. For example, if the child happens to knock over his drink, then it should be a matter of asking the child to rectify the damage and to clean up the mess or spill.

4. Loss of Privileges

If the child continues to push limits and not do as he or she is told, then the taking away of particular privileges is certainly appropriate.

5. Sitting Out from an Activity

Sitting out from a game or activity is a kind of mini time-out.

6 Time-out.

Time-out is the most effective means of punishing inappropriate or poor behavior.

7. Breaking the "Compliance" Rule

If you only needed to have one rule in the family, it would be the compliance rule. That's the rule that asks, "What do you do when Mom and Dad ask you to do something?"

This one rule underpins a good deal of your interactions with your child. What is the special procedure for if this rule is broken?

Review Time

Conclusion

CHAPTER 6

ADDITIONAL 17 HINTS

Your dreams and goals about having beautiful children who are happy and independent will not happen by accident. As we have seen in the previous chapters, you need to have thought about your parenting and to have actually planned how you are going to do this thing called parenting.

However, there certainly are some additional hints that may come in handy in relation to raising your children. These hints are outlined below.

Some of them you may indeed agree with, others you may not.

That's OK, just take what you think will work for you and use it, and those that you think are inappropriate, simply discard. You know in your heart of hearts what is going to work for you.

1. Tell Them that You Love Them – All the Time

When a baby is first born, there is almost a sense of unconditional love poured out upon this child. The baby can burp, bring up its food, dirty its diaper (and they have really, really smelly diapers), dribble everywhere and the baby still gets love and adoration. The parents or care-givers keep giving and giving and giving and the baby keeps taking and taking and taking.

However, somewhere along the line, the tolerance levels on the part of the parents tends to wear thin.

Whether it starts to wane around 6 months, 12 months or 2 years is a moot point – the fact is that the love appears to become more conditional.

"You be a good boy for Mommy and don't wet your pants;" "If you eat all your food, Mummy will give you a special sweet;" "If you don't stop crying, Daddy won't play with you."

Not surprisingly, the child gets the message that somehow or other, **he or she is not measuring up and not being good enough**. We all know that feeling. It has happened to all of us in some proportion.

Therefore, tell your children daily that you love them no matter what.

They need to hear it because much of what you do and say may be interpreted or perceived by your child as evidence that you do not love her any more. Unfortunately, this can happen. **You must do everything, therefore, to reassure your children that they are loved and tell them openly and clearly.**

If that feels awkward for you, then I only have one piece of advice. Get over it!

The world is littered with people who are emotional casualties because they have never heard their parents tell them that they loved them. Children yearn for it (don't we all). They hope for it and their heart screams for it.

Some parents will argue, though, that their children "know" that they are loved because of the sacrifices being made for them and the way in which they are looked after and cared for. Nice try, but it's not enough!

Children need to hear you say, "I love you." You need to say it. They need to feel it.

2. Try to Give Your Child Four Hugs a Day

We all need hugs. In an age that is definitely high tech, we certainly need to be high touch.

In other words, hugs are important for our mental and emotional health. We need to feel close and we need to feel connected. We need to feel as though we count and we need to feel special.

This means both parents. Both parents hugging their children. Hopefully, the parents also hug each other and provide the important modeling for their children. Remember, what you do is more potent than what you say.

Hopefully too, the hugging never stops. When your children are adults, hugging is still appropriate.

This is not some new age "trendy" thinking. This is reality. Your actions in the giving of a hug are louder than your words will ever be.

3. Remember to Practice What You Preach

It is not a case of "what I say" and "what I do" being two different things. Your modeling and who you are as a person are more powerful than what you preach.

In this respect, words are cheap.

Your child will learn more from watching you than anything that you actually say or try to teach.

If you read, for example, your child will often also read. If you exercise, your child will often exercise too. If you leave your clothes on the bathroom floor along with your wet towels, then don't be surprised when your child does the same. If you watch television for four hours a night, don't be surprised when your child also becomes a couch potato.

There is a saying that probably says it all, **"You have to lead from the front, not push from behind."**

4. Monitor the Television, Videos & DVDs

I remember reading once that **"the art of conversation was hidden behind the television set."** This is true for many families.

Don't allow the television to be on in the mornings when children are trying to get ready for kindergarten or school. You will lose as the parent and the television will win. You cannot compete with the television.

Don't allow the television to be on during the afternoons or evenings unless children have specific programs that have been selected beforehand. Otherwise, families end up aimlessly sitting in front of the box and mindlessly watching programs that they perhaps would ordinarily not want to watch except for the fact that the television happened to be on.

Additional 17 Hints

Teach children how to be selective about their television watching.

As well as monitoring television programs, you need to be aware of what **videos or DVDs** your children are watching. This is particularly so when children go to visit at their friend's house or perhaps go for sleepovers.

One last point. As parents, the television or videos ought not to be used as a babysitting device. Sure, there are times when parents need some space so they can get to do other jobs or chores, but then don't complain that your child is watching too much television or copying what they see on the "box."

5. Do not allow your Children to Watch "The News" Programs especially if they are Graphic in Content

For many children, watching the nightly news program (that the parents enjoy watching) is highly inappropriate given the amount of crime, violence and negative images that are portrayed.

This world is scary enough without children having to be exposed to real life drama and violence on a daily basis via the television screen.

Some children are highly anxious and watching TV news coverage only heightens their general anxiety and makes them feel very insecure and frightened. This could mean that they might experience nightmares, sleep disturbance, not wanting to go to bed, waking up in the middle of the night and wanting to come into the parents' bed, be clingy, and not want their parents to be out of their sight.

At various times in world events too, there are often world catastrophes such as war, assassinations, earthquakes, floods and tsunamis (tidal waves) to name a few. On these occasions, television coverage tends to be extensive with additional reports, footage and interviews. Often times, if the event is particularly noteworthy such as the tsunami in South-East Asia, then TV coverage can last days with updates, live telecasts and in the spot reporting.

Although the parents may want to keep up-to-date with such events, their children should not view the news. Such a viewing could traumatize a child without the parents initially knowing.

It is important to understand that children's brains do not become "adult" brains until puberty, and therefore, *they cannot get such world events and catastrophes into perspective or proportion*.

For children up to about the age of **7 to 9 years**, such viewing ought **not** to be permitted. For other children who are somewhat more anxious in nature and temperament, it may well be not until they are **10 or 11 years** that they watch such events on television.

I have had various television and press reporters ask me, "What about children needing to face reality?" in relation to such world events. My response to such a question is to allow people to understand that children have vivid imaginations and are not logical in their thinking and reasoning as are adults.

Once children's thinking has developed (usually around puberty), then they have the mental equipment and ability to be able to discuss and think through such events and what it means for them as individuals. As we know, with adolescence, comes what we call hypothetical-deductive reasoning or abstract thinking where the person is able to consider the bigger questions and issues of life. Up until that time, it is not appropriate to expose your children to world events and crises on television.

6. Check How the Computer and the Internet are Being Used

In the same way that television needs to be monitored, in this day and age, it is now a case of deliberately checking on how your children might be using the computer.

In this way, it is important to review the kind of computer games that your children might be using or borrowing from others. Some computer games are to be applauded in that they extend the child's thinking and reasoning abilities while others should be banned in terms of their violence and aggression.

Furthermore, it is critical to review how the Internet might be used if your child has access to the World Wide Web. Again, some web sites are particularly helpful in terms of their knowledge and information whereas other sites are appalling with their violence, pornography and sexuality. It is therefore important to hit the "History" button in order to monitor the web sites that have been visited by your child. It is also important to purchase software that bans access to particular sites.

You also need to check what is happening for your children when they visit at their friend's homes.

All may not be what it seems and you need to remember that other parents may not have the same values or perspectives as you might.

I have seen a number of children previously who were traumatized by what they saw at their friend's house and as a result, experienced nightmares, sleep disturbance or felt guilty or who, alternatively, began to engage in experimental or abnormal behavior.

A simple conversation asking your child what they did at their friend's house and then enquiring further with some gentle prodding is all that is required. Keep in touch with what your child is doing (if you did however, find out something had occurred at the home of your child's friend, then you would need to decide whether to quietly prevent your child from going over to that home, or raise the situation with the other child's mother or father).

7. Dedicate One Night a Week to a Games Night

Try at least once per week to have the television or computer turned off where the family does other things such as reading and playing games together.

You'll be surprised at how much fun it is.

Having a night where the family plays a board game or plays charades, for example, is a chance to relax and actually get to know one another.

8. Laugh Often

It has often been said that humor is the best medicine. This is particularly so in families.

Learn to laugh and enjoy one another. More especially, as parents, learn to laugh at yourselves.
- What would it take for you to be more light-hearted?
- What would it take for you to play some harmless tricks and "carry-on?"
- What would it take for you to sing or dance around the place?
- What would it take for you to be spontaneous or act a little crazy?

Don't take yourself too seriously. **Lighten up**.

9. Share the Jobs Amongst the Children

Life is not a free ride and children need to understand that they have a part to play in keeping the family functioning and operating. Families don't just happen and things just don't get done; someone has to make it happen.

Let them understand, even when they are very young, that they have an important role to play, tasks to do, and that the family is depending on them to do it.

It may be setting the table or putting the trash out or feeding the dog or the goldfish, but it is all part of the process of families functioning together.

10. Never Insult or Ridicule Your Child

Swearing at your child or calling him or her names says more about you as a person than it does about them as children.

You're the one with the problem!

This kind of behavior is never acceptable. It is bad enough that adults do it to other adults, but inexcusable with your children.

If you have a problem with your temper and anger management, then go and get some counseling and some professional help.

Be man or woman enough to go and sort yourself out so you can be a better person, and then a better father or mother.

Your children need your praise, your adoration and your support. They need positive words and reassurance.

11. Every Child Needs an Adult Who is Crazy About Him or Her

This is often the role of a grandparent.

Sometimes it is the role of an auntie or uncle. It is an adult in the child's life who **loves that child unconditionally,** which is so important in the child's development.

This is the person who makes the child feel special, who believes in the child, who makes the child feel valued and respected. Of course, parents need to do this too, but in this respect, someone outside the family can participate in this process and when it happens, it is very powerful.

I know one child who responded to this mother when she said that she loved him with, "Yeah, but you're supposed to love me...you're my mom." However, when his favorite Auntie also said she thought he was wonderful and she loved him too, he was quite overcome.

This external person is the one who allows the child to believe in themselves for no other reason than the adult believes in him or her. This adult may well spoil the child, which is just fine because it is what the child needs, and what it does to a child's self-esteem is miraculous.

12. Try to Make Sure that the First Two Years of Schooling are Fabulous

These first two years tend to set the benchmark for a child's future schooling.

You want to make sure that they get off to a good start in terms of their education. Set a firm and positive foundation. At this early stage, you do not want to lay down any beliefs about schooling and education that are negative or work against your child's future learning and development.

For example, with each of my three children, I took the liberty of interviewing the school principal about the kind of teachers that they would be having in each of their first two years of schooling. In other words, I wanted a nurturing, loving kind of teacher who was prepared at times to call the children "darling" or "sweetheart," for example, and who was prepared at times to give a hug if the child was clearly distressed or upset.

My child, who I love dearly and who has been in a loving family environment for the first years of her life, is being handed over to an educational environment which, in the first instance, I want to ensure is as loving and as caring as it can be. This is my child and I will not have a teacher or school undoing the good work that has already been done or in any way destroying my child's self-esteem.

I have heard of too many kindergarten and junior primary school teachers who at best can be described as "screamers" who "rant and rave." The damage they do to children's self-esteem and to children's learning is monumental. These kinds of teachers have no place in any school. They should leave the teaching to those scores of other teachers who really know how to teach by being supportive and caring while the same time setting clear boundaries and structure.

"Ranting and raving" says more about the teacher's inadequacies and failures than anything else. Setting up a classroom program with clear rules and with rewards and incentives means that the class can run harmoniously.

If your child is unfortunate enough to be with a "ranting and raving" teacher, make an appointment with the school principal to address the problem. If the school, for whatever reasons, will not address the issue, consider enrolling your child elsewhere if you can.

13. Don't Focus on Your Parenting to the Exclusion of Your Relationship

Adults fall in love as easily as they fall out of love. You have to work at it.

No doubt, you worked "hard" at falling in love. In other words, you probably sent cards or letters to each other, phoned each other daily or regularly, saw each other frequently and gave each other surprises or gifts.

The tragedy however, is that **as parents become tied up in their parenting** (not to mention paying the mortgage and the other bills as well as trying to forge a career or gain promotions), **the marital relationship becomes neglected**.

Couples stop phoning, sending cards or letters, stop talking, and don't spend time with each other. Is it any wonder that the love dries up and they become "like ships passing in the night?"

Children's greatest security comes from their parents' relationship. I once remember reading a little saying on the back of a bus ticket which read, "The greatest thing a father can do for his children is to love their mother."

I know there are demands on your life as parents. It is a busy time and you seem to be stretched in all directions, but don't become so caught up in the demands of life that you forget to nurture the love in your relationship or marriage.

As a general rule, I advise parents to put in place their own schedule. For example, it is extremely important to consider the following:
- ➤ Try for a half-hour conversation a day either over pre-dinner drinks, or perhaps over supper once the children have gone to bed.
- ➤ Have one night a week that you spend together maybe down at the local café or perhaps the local hotel.

- Go away for a weekend once every few months. Try to arrange for the children to stay with the grandparents or arrange for a nanny or even take the grandparents with you on a weekend so they can baby-sit. But most of all, get away.

It is not only important for you as a married couple to have one night a week out by yourselves and to get away once every few months, but important for your children to understand that they can survive with others for a short period of time, and that you will come back and probably, it is true to say, they may appreciate you just a little more.

14. Arrange for an Anger Bag or Pillow

We all get angry at times and we all have our ways of releasing anger. As adults, perhaps we count from 1 to 10, perhaps we take a deep breath, perhaps we go for a walk around the block, perhaps we self-talk in our heads and get things into perspective. We do whatever works for us.

Children need outlets too. Remember that no amount of appealing to logic or sitting them down and quietly talking to them is really going to work when the child is all steamed up with smoke coming out of his ears.

Instead, children need to have a special place where they can go when they feel angry or frustrated. A good idea is to have a bean bag or pillow that they can pound and take their anger out on by either hitting it with their fist or hand.

Releasing the anger in this kind of physical way is much more effective because as we have discussed before, children are very much "see and do." It is certainly much more effective than them taking it out on you or other family members.

A final point. As parents, it is also your responsibility to help your children identify their feelings, especially when they are angry or annoyed. Ask them, "What are you feeling? When you feel this way, how does your head and body feel? Can you tell when you're starting to feel this way?" People who are in touch with their feelings are more connected to themselves and to others.

As well as identifying the feelings, parents need to assist their children in working out what made them angry. What was the trigger? What got you so angry or annoyed? If that happens again next time, how can you do it differently? What could you do instead? People who know their triggers and what sets them off are better prepared to deal with situations next time round.

15. Don't Argue in Front of the Children

Of course, there are going to be numerous times when as parents you do not agree with each other. That is just the nature of life. Perhaps it is about your parenting styles, about whether your children can or cannot do something, about whether they can or cannot go somewhere. Perhaps it is about other issues (e.g. money, the in-laws, social outings, arrangements etc).

However, it is not appropriate to air your battles in front of your children.

If you have to disagree with each other, then do so in private. Perhaps retreat to your bedroom to sort it out together, but do not openly do battle in front of the children. **You do not have to agree with each other, but you do have to be together**.

Sort out your troubles behind closed doors. But if it is behind closed doors, don't do it in the middle of the night when children are trying to sleep or worse still, wake the children up with your yelling and arguing.

Incidentally, one of the major factors that causes childhood depression is the constant fighting and bickering that can go on between parents. It is unsettling for children and gives them a real sense of insecurity.

16. Don't Waste Your Time Asking "Why" Questions

In a nutshell, children simply do not know. More often than not, adults do not always know why they acted in particular ways either. Generally, we often just act and then rationalize it all later and tell ourselves a "story" to justify our position.

In short, "Why" questions are generally futile questions.

These so-called "silly" questions include;
- "Why did you do that?"
- "Why do you speak to me like that?"
- "Why do you keep fighting with each other?"
- "Why can't you just behave?"
- "Why don't you grow up?"
- "Why can't you be good?"

Generally speaking, **dumb questions beget dumb answers** (this goes for adults too).

Besides, even if children knew exactly the answers to these why questions, who says that this means that they would then act appropriately and behave?

Instead, as has been outlined in the previous chapters, as parents, you set up some rules and if the rules are broken, then there is an immediate consequence. The time to discuss other choices of behavior is after the consequences have been applied.

17. Teach your Child that there is a Mind, Body, Heart…& Spirit

Psychology in the main has been very helpful in allowing us to understand ourselves, but in the same breath, it has done us a disservice by generally omitting a significant portion of who we are as individuals.

The tide in psychology seems to be turning as numerous books such as those by authors like Ken Wilbur titled *"Integral Psychology"* point us again to the notion that there is certainly more to us than just our minds and our body.

We are made up of four parts, as shown below.

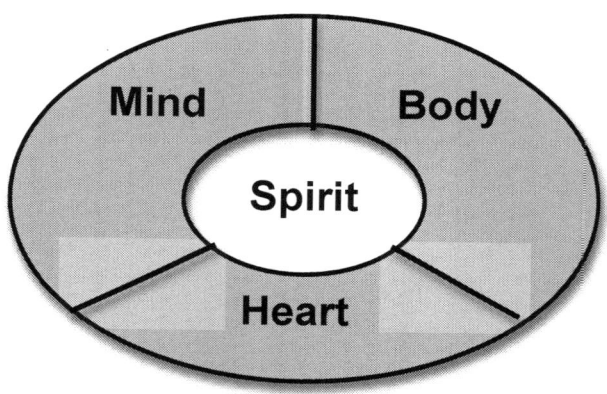

Now, to set the background here, the World Health Organization has predicted that **by the year 2020, 1 in 5 of our adolescents will be suffering from depression**.

Various writers have suggested that we will have an "epidemic" on our hands. I am not suggesting however, that the main feature in contributing to this apparent epidemic is the failure to recognize our spiritual dimension. Nevertheless,

I observe that those children and adolescents who acknowledge that there is another dimension called their spirit and that this dimension needs to be recognized and exercised, like we exercise our minds and bodies, seem to cope better overall.

This spiritual dimension is often exercised through meditation, through prayer, and through quiet daily reflection and reading.

Most of us, on the other hand, want to plug our day with noise, "busy-ness," "hurry-up-ness," pace and activity. We frequently try to juggle as much as we can.

Instead, the spiritual component is generally an individual experience which requires quiet, peace and stillness. It's amazing what comes to us out of the stillness — if we dare to stop and listen.

Some children and adolescents share their spiritual awareness through attending church or youth groups and camps and this, of course, is encouraged because it also means that they are learning to socialize, interact and communicate in yet another setting beyond school and family.

It is often out of this spiritual awareness that we find our mission in life, our purpose and our goal.

Every child (who will eventually turn into an adult) will one day ask the question, "What's my life's purpose?" Sometimes that question comes in the form of, "What's my contribution?", "How can I leave a legacy?"

It may not always be a conscious question, but it will be there.

"What's it all about?" "How does it all fit?" "What kind of job should I do?" "How can I be happy?" "Why am I here?"

The spiritual dimension cannot be underestimated.

CHAPTER 6 SUMMARY

1. Tell Them that You Love Them – All the Time

2. Try to Give Your Child Four Hugs a Day

3. Remember to Practice What You Preach

4. Monitor the Television, Videos and DVDs

5. Do not allow your Children to Watch "The News" Programs, especially if they are Graphic in Content

6. Check How the Computer, DVDs and the Internet are Being Used

7. Dedicate One Night a Week to a Games Night

8. Laugh Often

9. Share the Jobs Amongst the Children

10. Never Insult or Ridicule Your Child

11. Every Child Needs an Adult Who is Crazy About Him or Her

12. **Try to Make Sure that the First Two Years of Schooling are Fabulous**

13. **Don't Focus on Your Parenting to the Exclusion of Your Relationship**

14. **Arrange for an Anger Bag or Pillow**

15. **Don't Argue in Front of the Children**

16. **Don't Waste Your Time Asking "Why" Questions**

17. **Teach your Child that there is a Mind, Body, Heart...& Spirit**

CHAPTER 7

FREQUENTLY ASKED QUESTIONS

1. How do I help my child's self-esteem?

A healthy self-esteem is "life insurance."

Giving your child healthy self-esteem is, in my opinion, the most prized gift of all. Solid self-esteem is the buffer for all that life has to offer. It is the buffer that allows us to cope and counteract the effects of change. It allows the child (or person) to go with the flow rather than feel swamped by the changes going on around him or her. It allows us to cope more effectively with the stresses. It allows us to feel good about ourselves and more in control. We do not feel so much at the mercy of the "elements" as it were, where the winds and storms of life can beat down upon us at times.

So, where does self-esteem come from? How do we develop it? There are two keys to healthy self-esteem.

Self-esteem is both an "*outside*" job and an "*inside*" job. Let's discuss each one.

With the *"outside"* job, make sure that the following happens:

(1) You have a **strong behavior management program** where structure and routine is given to your child along the lines of what is discussed in this book.

(2) You need to **praise your children** and tell them what you appreciate. You need to give specific feedback such as "Thank you, Jane, for coming to the table when I called you, I appreciate that"; "Thanks for packing up your toys because it's really nice when the room looks neat and tidy"; "I really like it when you say please." You also need to give your child praise that is not necessarily dependent on a specific action like saying, "You are very special."

(3) You need to **find what your child is good at**. Is it drawing, dancing, playing sports, riding a bike or something else? If you don't yet know what talents your child has, find some and search for some. Then encourage that activity and make sure that you encourage it and support them. Being good at something is a major factor in assisting self-esteem at any stage of life, especially in the early childhood years.

(4) **Publicly display your child's achievements**. If, for example, your child gains a certificate or award from school, then post it on the fridge in your kitchen or put it on your display board. If your child gets a sticker from school, make sure it is displayed for all to see. Be prepared to put up photographs of your child playing sports, singing, playing a musical instrument, being in the school band or choir or whatever. Such reminders are powerful reinforcers of a child's strengths, talents and abilities and directly lift self-esteem. Especially is this so if visitors to the family or relatives, for example, happen to see such displayed and make comment.

> **"Seek first to understand, then to be understood."**
>
> Dr Stephen Covey
> USA Author & Consultant

(5) **Listen to your child.** One of the things that children and adolescents complain most vehemently about in the private confines of a psychologist's office or in the workshops that I conduct in schools is that parents do not listen. Of course, parents are very quick to point out that their children do not listen either. However, as an adult, it is important to model the kind of behavior that you would like to receive. In other words, if you want your children to be good listeners, then show them how to do it and practise it yourself.

Being listened to does wonders for self-esteem. It makes the individual feel important. It makes the child feel worthwhile and special. It makes the child feel as though she counts.

With the *"inside"* job, you need to attend to the following:

(1) **Monitor your child's self-talk** (also called "self-chatter" or internal dialogue). As Henry Ford wisely wrote, *"Whether you think you can or think you can't, you're right."* What you say in your head about yourself is critical to your self-esteem. For example, if you say things like:
- "I'm not good enough"
- "I'm dumb"
- "I'll never be any good at this"
- "I wish I was smart...good at sport ... pretty ... clever ... etc. etc."

...then how are you going to feel about yourself?

Not particularly good. Downtrodden. Second-best. You will feel as though you do not measure up and that somehow you have failed and no doubt, that others are better than you.

"What's one of the major differences between those who are successful and those who are not? The way they think."

(Darryl Cross)

If on the other hand, you say things like,

> "I may not know this skill right now, but I can learn it"
> "I may not have caught onto this, but with time, I know I can get it"
> "I may not be as pretty as [...put in a name...], but I know that I have other talents and besides, beauty is only in the eye of the beholder"

....then you'll feel better about yourself.

"Success doesn't come from the way you think it does; it comes from the way you think."

(Dr Robert Schuller; USA pastor & writer)

Is this just being pedantic? Is this just a play on words? Definitely not!

Your attitude or perspective is vital to the way you cope with life and handle whatever comes along.

> *"It's not your Aptitude; it's your Attitude that determines your Altitude."*
>
> (Zig Ziglar; Motivational speaker)

So, how do we monitor this with our children? You do two things. Firstly, **watch their moods and observe what they are doing**.

If they are showing any of the following:

- anxiety (uptight, nervous, stressed, tense)
- depression (feeling down, looking flat, sad)
- anger (annoyed, irritated, temper tantrums)
- guilt (feeling ashamed, embarrassed)
- resentment (feeling hatred and revengeful)

...then, it is possible that they have lost control of their thoughts and are saying things that are negative to themselves.

Alternatively, **your child will say out loud what he or she is thinking**. So do you as the adult.

When, for instance, your child puts him or herself down and says so out loud (e.g. "I'm hopeless," "I'll never be able to do it," What if I stuff up?" etc), you have a wonderful opportunity to correct that and give another way or perspective to help him see the situation.

A really good book that gives more information about children's self-esteem and the importance of self-talk is by Professor Martin Seligman and called *"The Optimistic Child."*

(2) **Create a positive picture in your child's "mind's eye."** In other words, we all think in pictures. Of course, we talk in words, but we actually visualise what we are saying in pictures and then describe it in words.

Are you aware that you actually do this? Think about it. You may do this so naturally and automatically that you never stop to think about it! Our language simply serves for us to describe the visualisations, pictures or videos that we have going on in our heads!

If this is so, how do we create positive pictures? Our children (like you and me) have pictures of themselves in their head anyway, so how do you make sure that those pictures are positive?

When children are young and you are putting them to bed, no doubt you might read to them, say prayers, have a little talk, have a cuddle or similar. This is a great time to tell them a positive story about themselves. Let them close their eyes and you tell them a story where they can imagine themselves doing well at sport, at school, making friends, drawing really well and all sorts of other activities.

In the same way, it's important in life to actually visualize how you would like to be personally and allow your children to do the same (e.g., being confident, happy, relaxed, successfully coping with school, getting on well with their friends). Tell them stories about how they are making friends at school, and how they are feeling confident and coping with whatever comes along. Let their little vivid imaginations see it all.

"Inferiority complexes are a myth; they are learned in childhood and believed right through life without any real evidence to support them."

(Darryl Cross)

Does this sound strange or somehow fabricated? It shouldn't, because this is what you and I do everyday and many of our stories are, in a sense, fabricated anyhow.

To take an extreme example, I maintain that inferiority complexes are always fabricated. In other words, inferiority complexes are made-up myths that we have sold to ourselves, where we have manufactured our own story. **Children are not born with inferiority complexes**. We create them. We make them up. We make up our own stories. We hallucinate. We spin ourselves a lie.

In life, there are two creations; first there is a mental picture, then there is the physical reality. No picture, no reality. That's just the way it is! So make sure that the pictures that you create for your children are positive ones and instead of leaving it to chance, actively allow your children to imagine positive stories of how they can behave and feel.

2. How do we help our children cope with the rapid change that is going on in our world?

What we need to acknowledge quite clearly is that the pace of change is not going to slow. If anything, it is predicted to get faster. **The one thing in life that is going to be permanent is change.**

Generally speaking, the "Seniors" in the community (those born before 1925), the "Builders" (those born between 1926–1945) as well as the "Baby Boomers" population (those born between 1946–1964) together with perhaps some of the early "Generation X" (born between 1965-1981), are all going to struggle with current change, which is now moving at an unprecedented rate.

Life was slower "back then."

The "Builders" for example, generally only had one, or at the most, two jobs in their lifetime, whereas the school leaver today can expect a minimum of 8 to 10 job changes and possibly 3 to 4 career changes.

In 1969, for example, did you know that there were only 4 computers in the world connected to what we know as the internet? Today, we have lost count, but it is certainly somewhere above 700 million computers on the Internet and growing each second.

All of these generations have had to cope with change without any real directions about how to manage and without any real training or instruction.

Somehow or other, we have gotten by. But, it is also true to say that there have been some very obvious casualties along the way in terms of "stress cases" due to retrenchments, restructuring, changing lifestyle, changing workplaces, and casualties with organizations and companies going bankrupt and falling over. There have also been the casualties in our families and in our relationships.

"If you put a frog in water and slowly heat it, the frog will eventually let itself be boiled to death. We, too, will not survive if we don't respond to the radical way in which the world is changing."

(Prof. Charles Handy;
"The Age of Unreason"

In short, I very much doubt that our globe has been prepared for the rapid change that we have seen over the last 30 years or so, particularly since the early or mid-1970s. Nevertheless, we have to cope with the change in order to survive.

How do we cope with change and allow our children to cope with it?

The answer lies in the following:

(1) Embrace and model change yourself

We are creatures of habit. We do things the same way.

We tend to do the same things in the morning when we get up, we tend to drive the same way to and from work, catch the same bus, eat in familiar cafes and restaurants, and shop in the same supermarket. We like routine. We like sameness and generally speaking, it makes us feel comfortable and makes us feel safe and secure.

> "Behold, the turtle only makes progress when it sticks its neck out."
>
> (Author unknown)

Instead, try to make change your best friend.

Drive a different way to work, or school and tell your children that you are doing so just for a bit of variety and for interest. Have a bit of fun with it. For example, if you take them to school, try to work out how many different ways there are for you to actually travel to school instead of taking the same route day after day.

In other words, model coping with change. Remember, it's not what you say that counts; it's what you do that counts. *(See the section, "The Power of Modeling" in this book.)* Your children are watching you. Be aware that they are always watching you.

So do things differently and try different things and tell your children that you are trying different things and let them see that it's okay.

(2) Encourage your children to take risks

Encourage them to take risks (even little ones).

We love to stay in what is called our "comfort zone." This is where we feel secure. But coping with change is all about stepping outside our comfort zone and into what is called our "courage zone."

Of course, don't expect your children to take risks if they see that you are too timid to do so yourself. If, for example, you are too timid to return damaged goods to the shop or too timid to seek information from the class teacher or school principal on a particular matter, then don't expect your children to be forthcoming in stepping out either.

"For you'd better start swimming or you'll sink like a stone, for the times they are a changing..."

(Bob Dylan; Pop singer)

Encourage your children to present themselves at the shop counter with money in hand to buy an ice cream or cool drink with you standing back and supervising. Let them answer the phone at home and teach them how to answer it correctly. Encourage them to answer the front door, providing of course, that you are present in the background supervising.

Remember too, to give them feedback, "Well done! You did it."

3. My child wets the bed; what do I do?

There is no doubt that this is a very common problem, which generally occurs more at night while the child is sleeping rather than during the day (i.e. most children are night wetters rather than day wetters). By the way, the professional term is "enuresis."

Clinically speaking, most of the children that I have seen who had a problem with wetting the bed at night had **usually been heavy sleepers**. They just hadn't learnt the skill of being able to recognize the signals that their bladder was full during the middle of the night and that they needed to empty it.

Of course, parents are often concerned that the bed wetting may be more an emotional problem rather than a purely physical problem, but in my experience, it has generally been the latter, in that children have just not learnt to physically register that their bladder is full and that they need a trip to the toilet.

Having said that, it is also true that on occasion, I have had some children present who have started wetting the bed again and this has been during a particularly stressful stage for them such as when parents are separating or divorcing, when there are problems during access visits, or for example, if there has been bullying at school.

The research shows that by about 4-years of age, around 75 percent of children are dry during both the day and night. After that point, the incidence of bed wetting reduces by about 20 percent per year. Generally speaking, it is considered important for the child to be dry both at night, and especially during the day, by the time he or she goes to school at five years of age.

Certainly, it has been my experience that the older the children get, the more severely it impacts on their self-esteem even if they are only night wetters. It means, for example, that they dread going on sleepovers; that school camps become fraught with anxiety for them, that family holidays become a major inconvenience when all sorts of precautions need to be taken.

What to do about it?

The first port of call would be a visit to your local doctor just to check that there is no obvious physical or medical explanation for the problem. Although some doctors do prescribe drugs to assist, the research suggests that medication is not particularly effective.

By far, the most effective treatment is the use of **a bed alarm**.

This works on the general principle that when the child wets the bed, an electric circuit is completed via a pad that sits under the sheet, and this causes a buzzing noise which prompts the child to wake up and go to the toilet. It is usually most successful in children over six years of age, but can also be very effective for younger children. Nevertheless, it is a prime means of teaching the child to be able to control his or her bladder.

These **pads and alarms** generally **come in two forms**.

Firstly, there is a **wrist alarm** that is attached by a cord to a clip that fastens onto the front of a child's underpants. These are often available from your local drug store or chemist, but are usually not as effective as the next option. Secondly, there is the more effective **bed pad and alarm** which can be rented or hired from some hospitals, community health centers or some psychologists who specialize in this area.

If there is one message that parents need to hear clearly in relation to bed wetting, it is to get on to it early, and try to ensure that the problem is alleviated by the time the child gets to school.

Frequently Asked Questions

4. We are separating in our relationship; how do we handle it with the children?

Unfortunately, in my experience, it is not so much the separation or the divorce that is the problem; instead, **it is the continuing battle (either covert or overt) between the mother and the father.**

Because of the breakdown between the parents in terms of communication and goodwill, and typically, because of the continuing anger and resentment towards each other, **the children get caught up in ongoing "guerrilla warfare."** The divorce or separation is painful enough for everyone, but it is a tragedy that it is really the ongoing warfare that damages children and is most destructive.

Such warfare need not be overt; **it can sometimes be covert through very subtle sabotage.** Separated or divorced parents by the nature of their situation and by the nature of their unresolved feelings continue to act in ways that hurt their children.

Above all else in this whole situation, what children have to know is that their mother or father is **not** abandoning them.

In short, it is the marriage or relationship that is broken, not parenthood.

Adam and Tim were two boys aged 9 and 11 years who sat in my office while their father waited for them in the waiting room. Their parents had separated about 20 months before and although there seemed to be an uneasy truce between Mom and Dad, these parents had seemed to communicate relatively well. At least they were able to work out access arrangements without too much drama or arguing.

> However, around 12 months previously, the divorce came through, and the father found a new partner about six months later. At that point, the relationship between the mother and the father soured significantly.
>
> The boys were now lost and confused. They loved their Mom and their Dad. These parents, however, were no longer talking to each other and, worse still, the boys felt trapped like they were "piggy in the middle". When they were at Dad's house, they did not feel that they were openly able to talk about what went on at Mom's house. To make matters worse, there was this woman at Dad's house and Dad was trying to pretend it was their mother. When they were at Mom's house, she was clearly angry most of the time or miserable and they heard quite clearly what a "bastard" Dad really was.
>
> I remember feeling somewhat sad for these two boys, but I remember smiling and saying to them, "It's really hard bringing up parents, isn't it?" A broad smile came across both their faces.
>
> There was a definite sense in which these two boys were being more parent in this situation than the two adults who were supposed to be rearing them.

Although some parents certainly fail in their marriage, it does not also mean that they need to fail in the divorce as well.

Few would deny that children thrive in a home where the mother and father love each other and love their offspring. However, marriages do end and no parent needs to feel that they have done their child irreparable damage if the marriage ends.

Therefore, what are the 10 tips that parents **must** adhere to in order to do all they can to assist their children in what is clearly an unfortunate situation?

Frequently Asked Questions

(1) Tell the children openly about the upcoming separation or divorce.

Many parents try to keep it a secret and put off telling their children, sometimes because of their own guilt and sometimes because they are trying to protect their children for as long as possible. The truth is, though, that children often know anyhow; they are good at picking up the vibes. Children are not easily fooled because they are acutely sensitive to what is going on between the two parents in the house. Their radar is supreme, so don't believe for a moment that they might be completely ignorant about what is going on.

What is important is that when you tell the child, do so in an open, understanding way. Your attitude will be critical. Let your children ask as many questions as they want and answer them simply and with reassurance. You don't have to go into intricate details unless the child pushes for some answers. Even if the situation is one of infidelity or one of abuse, you do not need to go into details (and maybe also try to score points against the other parent), instead, say that Mommy and Daddy are not getting on anymore or perhaps don't love each other any more.

(2) Tell the children that you still love them.

Children need to understand that although both parents are divorcing, the parents are not divorcing the children. Children must be reassured that they are still loved.

Because children have vivid imaginations, it is not unusual for them to automatically assume that their mummy or daddy doesn't love them as well.

(3) Reassure the children that they did not cause the breakup.

Again, it is not unusual for children to automatically assume that somehow or other they have caused the breakup in this relationship.

I still recall the five-year-old boy who was referred to me because of behavior problems. In the solitude of the psychologist's office, he sat on the edge of his chair looking down and confessed that his Mommy and Daddy broke up because he was "naughty and always getting into trouble." My heart went out to him. Nothing was further from the truth, and to see this little boy burdened with this guilt was a tragedy. Thankfully, once both his parents heard of his confession, they were quick to reassure him that he had nothing to do with their separation and impending divorce.

Having said that, I was seeing a 49-year-old male who generally had low self-esteem, who did not always communicate effectively and who tended to become angry rather quickly. He was still wearing the burden of the mother who clearly told him that his parents divorced because he was too much of a "handful."

To blame children for a separation or divorce is the cruelest of acts. Sure, they may have been difficult to handle (most children are), especially if the parents are too focused on themselves and their own problems. The breakdown in the marriage, though, is of the parent's making.

(4) Don't argue in front of the children.

Do not expose your children to your inadequacies in communication style. If you have issues with each other, then sort them out in private, such as in your own bedroom or after the children have gone asleep. Remember though, that your screaming at each other or even raised voices can be heard by children in their bedrooms at night and they tend to fret and blame themselves for the conflict. Perhaps instead, go and have a coffee together in the local restaurant, but do not rant and rave in front of your children.

Your children only serve to lose respect for you because of the things that you are likely to say and do when you are arguing. Often too, the things that you say in anger can be misinterpreted by your children. Outbursts such as "You're driving me insane" or "You're killing me" or "You're a complete loser" or "You don't care about anyone" can be taken literally by your children.

Furthermore, arguing only increases children's own tensions and anxieties and decreases their ability to be happy and enjoy life.

Research clearly shows that continual arguing and bickering has more impact on children than does the divorce itself. Research demonstrates that the leading factor for childhood depression is parent's arguing.

(5) Don't put down the absent parent.

This principle is probably one of the most common offences in divorcing couples. It seems to happen with such regularity, with again the children caught in the middle. Putting down the absent parent only serves to drag you down as well.

You may not love or like your departing partner and in fact, you may wonder why you ever chose to live with or marry him or her in the first place. Irrespective, it is critical to your child's development that they both love and respect each parent.

> Chloe was caught in the bitter struggle between her divorced parents.
>
> Her mother would constantly tell her how her father had simply abandoned them and as for maintenance or child support, he "didn't know the meaning of the word."
>
> In reality, I learnt that Chloe's father had been very generous in his monetary support and among other things had paid for all of Chloe's school fees.
>
> Inevitably, there was a sense in which Chloe felt betrayed by her mother.

From my own experience, it is clear that parents who criticize, put down, find fault (either subtly or openly) with the other parent only serve to end up destroying the relationship with their own children.

You reap what you sow. **Such criticism and fault finding will only come back to haunt you.** I have seen it time and time again. Every time you criticize the child's father or mother, you destroy a part of the child and the relationship that you have with him or her yourself.

> Jason's mother would often become angry and in her rage say things like "You're just like your father; he was a total loser too."
>
> Jason understood that his father had a number of issues including excessive use of alcohol and occasional gambling bouts. However, to be compared with his father in this way only served to confuse him and cause him to feel unhappy,

> and to question whether it might be true that he was, in fact, like his father.
>
> Over time, Jason came to understand that he could be his own person and that he did not have to be like his father, and that in fact he was not like his father.
>
> Nevertheless, the damage was done and he felt betrayed by his mother and ostracized from his father.
>
> He sought counseling in order to try to struggle with his own emotions and perspectives and as a way of understanding more clearly who he was and what he had to offer in life.

Don't fool yourself that you are "winning" and turning the children against their mother or father. Of course, parents who are fault finding and critical may think that they are influencing their child's opinion about the other party, but they are wrong. In the long term, they will not win because such criticism and bitterness will detonate their own relationship with their child and if anything, it is the parent who has been criticized who gains the greater respect.

(6) Don't force your child to take sides.

Parents need to know that in their best efforts to pull down the other party and force the children to be "on their side" only serves to work against them in the longer term. Such only serves to sabotage their own relationship with their children.

> **Don't fool yourself that you are "winning" and turning the children against their mother or father.**

If parents understood this, then they would never do these foolish acts.

Forcing children to take sides against a parent whom they love only causes them to feel anxious, guilty, resentful and trapped. Parents who demand this kind of allegiance alienate their children from themselves.

Jackson's father made it clear that the mother was "a whore" who left the family for a younger male and that she was "sex crazed."

Yet Jackson acknowledged that he still loved his Mom even though she had really hurt him and Dad when she walked out, but he said how difficult it was in that living with Dad, he had to be on "Dad's side." He couldn't bring up anything about his mother, he couldn't mention her name and if he went to secretly visit her, which he did on occasion, he was then not able to talk about the visit at all at home.

He had to conceal his innermost thoughts and feelings and he struggled at times to remain happy and keep his school grades up.

At times, he felt very alone and lost (little wonder!).

Demanding, too, that your children choose where they will live, either with the father or the mother, is ill considered and ill-advised.

Children love both their parents and should not be asked to choose. Of course, older children are often consulted about where they would wish to live, but for their own healthy development, it needs to be the parents or an external professional such as a psychologist who makes the decision. Such a decision and its consequences cannot be left with the child alone.

The big people in the child's life need to make such decisions.

(7) Don't suddenly change the child's routine.

Routine is security. It helps children know where they are and how they fit. They feel safe in routine.

Suddenly altering a child's routine is usually going to throw them out of orbit. If at all possible, ensure that your child stays in the same house, goes to the same school and plays with the same friends.

Some parents like to share the custody and access so that the children spend 50% of the time in one house and 50% of the time in the other house. That might be one week in one house and the next week in the other house or it might be one school term in one house and the next term in the other house. While this might work for the parents, in my experience, it rarely if ever works for the children. It is much more appropriate for the children to have a "home base" and to then spend particular nights or every second weekend or similar with the other parent. Otherwise, the "to-ing and fro-ing" between homes only serves to unsettle the children, who may feel that they really don't belong anywhere.

(8) Don't fight over access or visitation rights, either overtly or covertly.

Again, it is a case of children being caught in the middle. They didn't ask for this separation or divorce, but they become like pawns in a game between angry or resentful parents who either knowingly or unknowingly use their children to get back at the other parent, and to "score" against the other parent. One wonders who the "children" really are in this sort of circumstance.

Some of the ways that parents become vindictive includes **stopping the children from actually going on access visits**. This might occur, for example, if the father was behind in child support or maintenance payments or behind in paying the school fees. It may be so that one parent is hard to get along with, but denying the child the right to see the other parent is simply not appropriate. Whether one parent likes it or not, the children still have a father or mother who they need to see.

Restricting incoming phone calls is another ploy that some parents take. One mother, for example, would answer the phone and tell the father that the child was either busy or not at home. Alternatively, some parents might restrict outgoing phone calls. When a child asks if he or she can call to talk to their father, for example, the mother simply refuses, saying "no" and often without any further explanation. Remember, children need both parents and saying "no" or restricting calls is only going to build resentment against the restrictive parent.

Giving a child **"the third degree" following an access visit** is another ploy and a foolish one at that. The child is caught in a no-win situation. If she tells all about the access then she is being unfaithful to the absent parent and risks saying or doing things that irritate or anger the present parent. If she says nothing

Frequently Asked Questions

and withdraws, then she incurs the wrath of the present parent and gets accused of protecting the absent parent or perhaps gets accused of "not loving" the present parent. Don't put your child in a no-win situation.

Therefore, stay away from loaded questions such as:
- "Is your Mom going out with another man yet?"
- "What did your father say?"
- "Did you have fun today?"
- "Aren't you glad to be home?"
- "What did Daddy feed you?"
- "You didn't see your father's mother today, did you?"

These kinds of questions compromise you. They are all loaded questions. Asking your children to spy on their parent or be a confidant is simply not okay. Cut it out!

(9) The visiting parent needs to keep to any promises, times or dates that have been arranged.

If you are a visiting parent, and you have made arrangements to pick up your children or meet them at a particular time and place, then make sure that you **honor that commitment.** Of course, on occasions, emergencies do arise, but these do not happen often and generally the child understands such events.

However, simply not turning up or changing arrangements at the last minute is a definite "no – no." Your son or daughter will only interpret this as you not caring or loving them. I have certainly seen occasions where this has precipitated a clinical depression for some children.

You as a parent need to be a person of your word. After all, that is where trust comes from. If for example, your children cannot trust you to turn up and be on time, then how can they trust you with any other arrangements or things you might say?

(10) If you are the visiting parent, do not try to buy your children's love.

The offending parent in this regard, at least in my experience, tends to be the father.

It is not unusual to see a father who is attempting to buy his children's love through not only giving them a good time while on access with unlimited food, drink and entertainment, but also showering them with gifts, including promises of future gifts and presents.

Some parents unfortunately act in this way for various reasons. The absent parent might be feeling guilty and this is one way of trying to appease their own feelings of guilt. Alternatively, the strategy of showering the children with gifts or indulging them can sometimes be a means of trying to show up the other parent. Such indulgences are misguided. It only teaches children to be manipulative. In other words, children are not silly and they work out with which parent they can have a meaningful relationship and trust and they work out which parent they can manipulate in order to gain gifts and other material needs. The parent who does the overindulging obviously believes that somehow or other this strategy is working by satisfying both the parent's need as well as the child's needs.

It is a shallow strategy. It might make the parent feel a tad better, but it does nothing for a real relationship with the children. Don't fool yourself that this is a winning strategy. It isn't.

In the short term, the indulgent parent may think they are in front, but on the longer term overindulgence does nothing for the relationship that you really want with your children.

5. My child said that he wished he was dead; what should I do?

"I wish I was dead," "I want to kill myself," "I want to die." Sometimes children say these things and typically, it freaks parents out. So, how seriously should you take it? What should you do (if anything) about it?

Is it really real?

The first thing you have to work out as a parent is if the comment from your child is really honest. Could it just be that he or she is actually annoyed at you, wants to pay you back, wants to get even, wants to make you feel guilty? This, of course, is still of a concern, but it is not life threatening.

Many of us can probably recall when we were younger and really ticked off with Mum or Dad, saying in the heat of the moment things like, "I'm going to run away," "You'll miss me when I run away," "I'm going to live with...," "You'll never see me again." I can remember saying some of those things and so can many of you. Heck, it was the only way we knew how to hit back.

How do you tell if it is really real?

Look for other signs that the child is unhappy or sad in some way. For example:
- Do they consistently mention that they are unhappy?
- Do they often say that they wish they were dead?
- Have they often thought about dying?
- Are they troubled by these thoughts?
- What is it that makes them sad or unhappy?

The answers to these questions help determine the seriousness of the feelings of general sadness or unhappiness.

At a wider level too, it might be important to ask:

- What is happening in the family?
- Are Mom and Dad also troubled and unhappy?
- How are the parents coping with their own problems?

The answers to these questions help to determine whether the child might simply be mirroring the parents' emotions and concerns rather than being caught up in his or her own private issues.

Which children seem to be more susceptible to suicidal talk?

In my experience, I have noted a pattern in the kinds of children who present for help with these kinds of thoughts. For example, they tend to be the following:
- Intelligent or bright
- Deep thinkers
- Introverted and inward looking
- Very sensitive
- Have a vivid imagination

What situations seem to trigger off this kind of talk?

While it is true to say that frequently, for the kind of child described above, there is no specific trigger or situation that sets off suicidal talk, it is also true that the sorts of situations listed below can activate feelings of hopelessness and unhappiness:

- a learning problem at school, or dyslexia
- no friends at school or being teased or harassed
- believing that the teacher is picking on them or doesn't like them
- parents fighting or constantly arguing
- believing that the parents favor a brother or sister and not them
- a death in the family or the extended family (e.g., grandparents)

- illness for the child or prolonged illness of a family member
- living in a troubled family
- living with verbal, emotional or physical abuse

What to do about it?

If your child is in a secure, loving environment, then ask yourself, why is this happening? Why is your child saying these kinds of things? Even if you consider that your child might be simply trying to get back at you or somehow you believe is trying to manipulate you, it is important to focus upon what they have said.

If you are concerned, as no doubt you would be, then find an opportunity to bring it up with your son or daughter. **Above all, react in a calm, matter-of-fact voice**. Do not sound alarmist because you certainly don't want to exaggerate the situation.

It may be appropriate to discuss it at the instance that they say it, providing of course, that others are not within ear-shot and that you are alone. Otherwise, it might be appropriate to bring it up when you are tucking him or her into bed at night and there is a quiet, intimate time for the two of you. You will at some point though, need to bring it up because you need to know what is going on.

You may also subtly ask the teacher how your child is doing at school. Have they noticed anything? How is your child doing academically? How is she getting along with others? You may also gently enquire of your neighbors, friends etc. with whom your child associates as to whether they had noticed anything. **You don't have to be candid about your enquiries – you don't want to create a problem if there is not one there in the first place!**

If you believe, all things considered, that there are some genuine concerns, then approach a psychologist or psychiatrist for an appointment. Possibly, you may wish to attend the first appointment alone. If your child is in distress, however, he or she will often ask to see someone or you could suggest that you go together to talk about their unhappiness.

I have often had parents tell me that in the first instance, children say that they do not want help or assistance, but it is only a matter of weeks or months later that they ask to see a professional or ask for counseling. More often than not, they tend to simply say, "Mom and Dad, I need help" or "I need to see someone."

6. My child has been very aggressive; is it just a phase that he is going through?

Aggression at any time ought not to be tolerated. What we are talking about here is verbal aggression such as swearing, and bad-mouthing the parents or siblings; physical aggression towards others such as hitting, biting, kicking, spitting usually directed towards the siblings or parents; physical aggression towards things such as breaking or destroying toys including their own as well as those of the siblings.

More particularly, if the aggression has been over a number of months and longer than say, six months, then there ought to be concern on the part of the parents. I have often heard parents suggest that when their children are difficult to get on with or are argumentative, aggressive or angry, that it's "just a phase that they're going through." Such a comment really is a cop out. Phase or no phase, it needs to be dealt with immediately.

From a psychological perspective, it needs to be recognized too that generally speaking, aggression is an instinctive reaction to when a person feels unsafe, cornered or perhaps worthless.

At one end of the spectrum though, we have children who are simply testing the limits and boundaries to see how much they can get away with. For example, they might throw temper tantrums or perhaps be aggressive towards their siblings with hitting or yelling or kicking or they might even destroy their siblings' toys or possessions or even their own possessions.

Sometimes, children just might try it on to see where the limits might be. Sometimes, they might simply be modeling the aggression that they have witnessed in the household or from the parents themselves.

It needs to be said quite clearly though, that if one or both parents are verbally or physically aggressive, then such **modeling is a powerful influence**.

As parents, it is simply not reasonable to expect your children to do one thing while you do another. In other words, parents need to ensure that their own behavior in the first place is acceptable and appropriate and that they model good behavior for their children, including anger management.

However, assuming that parents are setting the appropriate role model, then instituting the behavioral program that is discussed in this book is a good place to start to immediately intervene with this kind of aggression.

To reiterate, firstly, the parent needs to set the rule about the kind of behavior that is acceptable. For example, a rule to curb aggression might be, "Share and play nicely with your brothers and sisters" or "Speak calmly and politely to others in the family."

Secondly, the rule has been set out and has been clearly posted on the fridge or on a pin-board or somewhere obvious.

Thirdly, the parent then needs to both reinforce and reward the rule being kept (i.e. give out tokens) and punish or penalize (i.e. send to time-out) if the rule is broken.

On the other hand, and at the other end of the spectrum and generally because of specific factors such as a chaotic family situation, family violence, poor parenting, drug and substance abuse, child neglect, parental depression, and parental psychiatric disturbance, around 5 to 10% of children can be considered to have moderate to severe behavioral problems. This includes being aggressive and violent (e.g. they swear, yell, fight, pick on others, are non-compliant, destroy property, are disruptive in class and are uncontrollable).

What is really important to understand about this minority of children is that if parents (and schools) do not intervene and fix the problem (and sometimes with the help of a professional such as a psychologist or social worker), then the research shows that these aggressive, violent, anti-social children are simply going to move into juvenile delinquency and adult offending. This is critical to understand and I have written about this elsewhere (Cross, DG. et al., "Conduct-Disordered Children: A Review", Records of the Adelaide Children's Hospital, 1985-86, Vol. 3, No.3, p.244-257).

As we well know, the leopard finds it very difficult to "change its spots." The Jesuit saying puts it well, "Give me a child until he is seven and I'll show you the man." The poet John Milton wrote in 'Paradise Lost', "Childhood shows the man as morning shows the day" (they were written a long time ago and are sexist sayings, but the message is still very clear). Put another way, trying to turn around a horse when it has bolted is very difficult.

Early intervention with these children is the key. Unless direct treatment intervention is applied in the early years, it is highly probable that the child's disruptive behavior will persist over time.

**Early intervention is the key.
Don't allow this kind of behavior to continue.**

This will evidence itself later in delinquency, and still later in adult adjustment antisocial disorders with a consequent astronomical cost to the community in terms of welfare, law and order resources, insurance payouts and premiums, and compensation.

Such treatment or intervention programs would involve the following kinds of components:

> **1.** Arrange for parents (or the caregivers) to receive counseling on basic parenting skills and how to manage and care for children.
> **2.** Provide continual and hands-on behavior management support for the classroom teacher.
> **3.** Have a consultative group of medical specialists and pediatricians, educators and allied health professionals like psychologists and occupational therapists who can provide expert assessment and advice on child issues as necessary.
> **4.** Provide a withdrawal unit staffed with a multi-disciplinary team of teachers, special education teachers, psychologists, social workers, and family therapists.
> **5.** Arrange for the behavioral children to be taken each day to the withdrawal unit where they would receive a tailored program focusing on their educational needs, social skills and personal issues requiring individual counseling.
> **6.** Have withdrawal units shared between small groups of schools or ideally, a unit set up within every school.
> **7.** Train the classroom teacher in skills to handle the child once he/she is placed back into the mainstream classroom.
> **8.** Ensure that there is continual follow-up and support provided to the classroom teacher, the parents and the school.

In a nutshell, **it is too late once the horse has bolted**.

Whether your child is just "trying it on," whether your child is feeling vulnerable and unsafe, whether your child has a severe behavioral problem or whether your child is somewhere in between, deal with the aggression immediately irrespective of whether you believe it is a "phase" that he or she is going through.

7. I feel so stretched as a parent; is it OK for me to take time out?

We all need time out at various stages. Taking time out is not the issue. What is important, though, is how you do it and how it is communicated to your children.

Threatening, for example, that because of your children's behavior, you are going to leave home or run away (or worse still, kill yourself) is simply **not** acceptable.

These kinds of threats are appalling and create major damage to your children's sense of security and self-esteem, not to mention their relationship with you and the trust they have in you.

Anna presented as a single mother who was struggling to cope with her son and daughter who were aged 5 and 7 respectively.

She talked about the difficulties of being a single parent and said that basically she felt that the job was beyond her.

She knew she was struggling, but what had triggered her making an appointment for assistance in her parenting were the threats that she was now delivering to her children; saying things like she would simply walk out and leave them if they didn't behave.

She said she knew she should not say these things and she looked quite forlorn and distraught as she recalled the image of her children's faces and the fear and terror that they obviously experienced when she made this threat.

If you need to take time out, such as going away for a weekend to perhaps visit friends or have your own retreat, then plan it carefully and ahead of schedule. Do not suddenly institute such a trip in a moment of crisis because you have to "get out."

Make sure you give everyone, especially your children, prior warning that you will be away for a brief period. Importantly, let your children know that they will be cared for and looked after by someone who they trust and love such as an aunt and uncle, grandparents or close family friends.

In this way, children will learn that they can get on without you and that they can survive without you being on-call for them 24 hours a day. Absence makes the heart grow fonder and being away for a few days may even help them to appreciate you a little bit more. In these kinds of circumstances, your planned period away can be a win-win situation.

8. What about family conferences?

Life in this century seems to becoming busier and busier, and with it, there seems to be less and less time for those around us, including talking and conversing with those in the same house.

Parents, for example, tend to become caught up in the hustle and bustle of life, which includes forging a career, paying the mortgage and dealing with the children. There is a sense in which these pressures have always been there, but in recent times, these trends seemed to have increased.

Yet, the family is still the foundation of our society where we learn to talk, to share, to grow and to learn who we are in interaction with others.

One sure way of ensuring that the family does make time to communicate is to organize what is called a **"family conference."** Of course, communications among family members is meant to happen informally and naturally, but the nature of 21st Century life now means that it may be important to program in special communication time.

Perhaps it may seem artificial to formally program in this time, but life is such now that if a family conference is not formally arranged, then typically the communication and liaison that is absolutely necessary for effective family functioning tends to be lost and disappears.

Family conferences are also a great way to model to your children how families ought to communicate and how everyone "having their say" is an important dynamic for life itself.

A family conference, therefore, is really nothing more than everyone in the family putting aside a specific time to talk together. They are usually held once per week. Family conferences are sometimes scheduled on a regular night, or can be variable depending on the availability of family members, especially the parents.

What happens at a family conference?

A number of approaches can be taken.

Families can take the opportunity to talk about how things are running generally. Are the family routines working well? If not, why not? What needs to happen to ensure that the family is running well? Are there any "hot spots" in the family where people are unhappy with each other? What would you like to see this family do more of? What would you like to see this family do less of?

Families can also take the opportunity to "get to know each other" better. This might sound strange because families are supposed to know each other living under one roof, but often, nothing is further from the truth. So, in terms of an exercise, each family member can provide positive feedback about the other family members (e.g. What do I like best about each person? What are each member's strongest points? What is the nicest thing that each member has done for me?) The family members take it in turn to receive this kind of feedback and the family moves systematically around the group giving their comments to individuals.

Perhaps a variation on a theme can also mean that the family conference might organize a games night one week, as previously mentioned. Board games, charades or any other kind of fun night is certainly appropriate. Families need to have fun together. Not only is important to talk together, but to laugh together.

Family conferences may seem a bit way out to some parents. Nevertheless, give it a trial. You may be surprised at how well they work and what you may learn about each other as well as how it strengthens family bonds and relationships.

If you decide that family conferences are "not for you," then it is important to create regular opportunities for family chat time such as at the table after family meal.

9. What parenting tips are there for fathers?

Research, as well as anecdotal experience, shows that fathers are increasingly becoming involved with child rearing and parenting. For example, census data shows that 30 years ago only 1% of fathers were attending at their children's birth whereas today that figure is now around 80%.

Traditionally speaking, fathers have often performed a number of roles in relation to being a parent. For instance, there is the role called the **"Lord of the Manor"** where the spouse and everyone else are slaves, the children are seen and not heard and the father dishes out punishments / pardons.

Then there is the role of the **"Fault Finder"** who is full of put downs and nit-picking, non-supportive, and highly critical, where the children can't do anything right.

Next, there is the role of **"Norm" Father** who gives up all responsibilities / power to the wife / mother, and who backs down on everything (something like Bart Simpson's dad) and who often retreats into alcohol, television, the newspaper and / or the garden shed.

Finally, there is the **"Never at Home" Father** who is off making a career and a name for himself (plus money). He is early to work and late home, can often be away for extended periods, brings work home, and never or rarely manages to attend children's sports, school events or functions.

These old roles are yesterday's. As I said before, fathers are much more involved in their parenting than they ever have been.

In brief, fathers would do well to remember and implement the following 5 tips:

1. Be positive and give praise. Make a point of doing this and not, as I've said before, for the big things that might occur such as coming top of the class for a test, of throwing the winning goal, but instead, praise needs to be daily for all the little things that occur (e.g., coming to the table when called, taking their dish to the kitchen sink etc.).

2. Listen to the children. Really listen and feed back what you have heard. This means being active in listening and not just the occasion "uh huh" or grunt.

3. Have consistent rules and routines. See Chapter 3 titled "*The Rules Wheel.*"

4. Spend time. Be with them. As has been said before, there are no short-cuts in this child raising business.

5. Take / share in the roles / chores of parenting. This is a combined process between two parents (providing of course, that you're not a single parent). You both had a hand in bringing your children into the world. Share in the process.

10. How do I help my shy child?

It is certainly true that some children are born extroverted (estimated around 60% in countries like Australia to 70% in the USA) and some children are born introverted (around 40% and 30% respectively). Extroverted children who tend to be more outgoing and gregarious find it easier to mix with others and make friends. Because they get more practice at it, they tend to have better social skills and often end up being leaders.

However, on the other hand, the more introverted children are slower to make friends, are more reticent to move into groups and can often hang back from interactions. If anything, while the extroverts tend to have a large circle of acquaintances, the introverts tend to have one or two friends and often have them for life.

All this goes to say that if your child is an introvert, then it is certainly possible that she may take longer to make friends and move into a group. In this way, you as a parent will need to set up opportunities for your child to connect one-on-one with other children.

It is generally not successful to place an introverted child into a group and hope that he or she makes friends. Instead, arrange for your child to invite a friend over to play for a few hours. Make sure, though, that it is one-on-one. This gives introverts the best chance to be able to relate and connect. Do not invite a number of friends over because what will generally happen is that the introvert gets left behind in the games and interactions that occur.

Make sure too, that as parents, you again model appropriate social skills and show your children how to openly relate and communicate. This also means being bold in your interactions irrespective of who you are talking to and that you are not giving any messages that somehow or other you might be inferior or that others might be superior and have the upper hand.

The reason for your child's shyness may not simply be that he is introverted in nature. Instead, he may have low self-esteem and lack confidence socially. He might be worried about what other boys and girls might say and do to him and he might get embarrassed easily.

If your child has a problem with feeling worthwhile and lacking esteem, then I refer you to the first question in this chapter titled, "How do I help my child's self-esteem"?

"To value his own good opinion, a child has to feel that he is a worthwhile person. He has to have confidence in himself as an individual."

(Sidonie Gruenberg)

CHAPTER 7 SUMMARY

1. How do I help my child's self-esteem?

Giving your child healthy self-esteem is the most prized the gift of all. Self-esteem is both an "outside" job and an "inside" job.

With the *"outside"* job, make sure that the following happens:
  (1) You need to have a **strong behavior management program**
  (2) You need to **praise your children** and tell them what you appreciate
  (3) You need to **find what your child is good at**
  (4) You need to **publicly display your child's achievements**
  (5) You need to **listen to your child**

With the *"inside"* job, you need to attend to the following:
  (1) Monitor your child's **self-talk**
  (2) Create a **positive picture** in your child's "mind's eye"

2. How do we help our children cope with the rapid change that is going on in our world?
  (1) Embrace and model change yourself
  (2) Encourage your children to take risks

3. My child wets the bed; what do I do?

By far, the most effective treatment is the use of a bed alarm.

4. We are separating in our relationship; how do we handle it with the children?

Above all else in this situation, what a child or children have to know is that their mother or father is **not** abandoning them. The 10 tips that parents **must** adhere to are:

(1) Tell the children openly about the upcoming separation or divorce.
(2) Tell the children that you still love them.
(3) Reassure the children that they did not cause the breakup.
(4) Don't argue in front of the children.
(5) Don't put down the absent parent.
(6) Don't force your child to take sides.
(7) Don't suddenly change the child's routine.
(8) Don't fight over access or visitation rights, either overtly or covertly.
(9) The visiting parent needs to keep to any promises, times or dates that have been arranged.
(10) If you are the visiting parent, do not try to buy your children's love.

5. My child said that he wished he was dead; what should I do?

Alleviate your fears as a parent by checking the answers to the following questions:
- Is it really real?
- How do you tell if it is really real?
- Which children seem to be more susceptible to suicidal talk?
- What situations seem to trigger off this kind of talk?
- What to do about it?

6. My child has been very aggressive; is it just a phase that he's going through?

Whether your child is just testing the limits, or has a severe behavioral problem or somewhere in between, deal with the aggression immediately irrespective of whether you believe it is a "phase" that he is going through.

7. I feel so stretched as a parent; is it OK for me to take time out?

Yes. Taking time out is not the issue. What is important, though, is how you do it and how it is communicated to your children.

8. What about family conferences?

Family conferences may seem a bit way out to some parents. However, you may be surprised at how well they work and what you may learn about each other as well as how it strengthens family bonds and relationships.

9. What parenting tips are there for fathers?

In brief, fathers would do well to remember and implement the following 5 tips:

(1) Be positive and give praise. Make a point of doing this.
(2) Listen to the children. Really listen and feed back what you have heard.
(3) Have consistent rules and routines. See chapter 7.
(4) Spend time. Be with them.
(5) Take / share in the roles / chores of parenting.

10. How do I help my shy child?

If your child just happens to be more introverted in nature, then only invite one friend or child over to play for a few hours at a time. If your child happens to have low-self esteem, then refer to the information provided in question one of this chapter.

CHAPTER 8

FREQUENTLY ASKED QUESTIONS ABOUT CHILD DEVELOPMENT AND SCHOOL

1. How do I know if my child has a Specific Learning Disorder or Dyslexia?

Before we go any further, let's understand what a specific learning problem is and what dyslexia is. *Are these labels different*? Essentially, no.

Dyslexia is the popularized term seen in the local media and the press. It actually means "difficulty with words" and traditionally has referred to difficulties with the written form of language or with "words in print."

Therefore, Dyslexia originally referred to a reading disorder. Other disorders, for example, included dysgraphia (writing) and dyscalculia (problems with arithmetic). Over time, however, these and a variety of other difficulties have been generally subsumed under the one label of "Dyslexia."

Specific Learning Disorder (SLD), therefore, emerged more recently over time as an umbrella term which described the range of disorders which seem to affect learning. Generally, though, both terms are now often used interchangeably, although Specific Learning Disorder is the more recent and preferred term.

What is a Specific Learning Disorder or Dyslexia?

It is generally believed that specific learning disorders are due to a neurological or cognitive weakness; in other words, a small part of the brain is not processing information appropriately. In particular, it has been suggested that with a learning disorder, the following could be the issue at hand:

* The disorder *is in one or more of the individual's basic processes* (such as auditory or visual memory, sequencing ability, visual-motor processing, phonological awareness).

* The individual has *difficulty in learning*, specifically in relation to speaking, listening, reading, writing or mathematics.

* The disorder is *not primarily due to other causes* such as visual or hearing impairments, motor handicaps, mental retardation, emotional disturbances, or economic, environmental or cultural disadvantages (however, one or more of these can also occur along with learning disabilities).

* A *severe discrepancy* exists between the individual's apparent potential for learning and his or her actual achievement levels.

* It is to be noted that an individual with a specific learning disability still falls within the *normal intelligence* range; that is, he or she does not fall within the intellectually or mentally deficient range.

How Common Is It?

Did you know that roughly 10% of students have a learning problem such as dyslexia? Statistically speaking, the frequency of a specific learning disability in the population varies from around 3% to 15%. That means there are somewhere around one to three students in every classroom with dyslexia. We are not talking about a rare or unusual problem. We are talking about a very common issue that unfortunately, gets swept under the carpet and overlooked.

It is also more common amongst boys. The ratio is about 5:3, for boys versus girls, but it may also be that boys may come to the teacher's notice more readily.

Unfortunately, governments since the early 1970s have progressively cut back on funding for students with genuine learning disorders or dyslexia. Unfortunately, not all teachers are trained sufficiently in being able to identify dyslexia and sadly, many students get pushed through the system ending up with poor self-esteem and feeling a failure because they had dyslexia which had gone un-recognized and undetected.

One of the saddest parts of the job of being a psychologist is to see fine young men and young women in Grades 9 to 12 in high school or secondary education who present with behavioral problems, or who are withdrawn and depressed, and with low self-esteem who have dyslexia that has not been picked up through the education system.

It is indeed a tragedy and sad for countries that are supposed to be advanced and some of the world leaders in terms of education.

How Do You Recognize Dyslexia?

There are several common characteristics of learning problems, but is it unlikely that a student would show all of them. Some of the "tell-tale" signs of learning difficulties are as follows:

- short concentration span, easily distracted, not following instructions, forgets things
- daydreaming
- poor coordination, poor or untidy handwriting, slow in writing things down or copying
- seems to be about average or above average in intelligence, but behind in areas such as math, spelling, reading and writing
- delayed speech or difficulty with language
- poor behavior such as being disruptive in class, annoying others, "class clown"
- poor organizational skills, loses books, pens etc.

Why Does it Occur?

Clinically speaking, there are primarily **three main reasons** why it occurs:

(1) **Heredity**. One of the parents, or someone in the extended family, has a similar problem. Often when I am explaining the test results of an assessment on a student with dyslexia, one parent such as the father might say something like, "I think you're talking about me when I was a boy at school" or "That's exactly like me" or "That's how I was when I was at school." At other times, the parents will say that there is dyslexia in the family and that one or the other of the grandparents had dyslexia or that an uncle has dyslexia.

(2) **Problems in the pregnancy**. In this case, the mother might explain that there were some complications during the pregnancy or that she was hospitalized early before the birth or similar.

(3) **Problems at birth**. Often the mother will say something like, "The cord was tied around his neck when he was born and he didn't get enough oxygen at first, but we were told he'd be fine."

Again, clinically, it is our experience in a psychology practice that around at least 60-75% of clients can trace the problem back to their family genes. For some cases, though, there does **not** seem to be an obvious reason.

Can it be Cured?

Because it is basically a brain processing problem, it has been present essentially from birth and so, along with the rest of our features (e.g. eye color, skin color etc.), what we have got, we have got!

But, as with most of us, we learn to work around our so-called difficulties – none of us are perfect. With dyslexia, we work around the problem by organizing special programs, teaching formats and aids.

Are All Learning Difficulties Caused by Dyslexia?

There are a number of forms of dyslexia, but it is certainly true to say that not all learning problems are dyslexia. Children all learn at different rates, for example, and some can be slower than others to catch on and pick up and process material.

Some children are what could be termed "Slow Learners" which means that although in some areas they might show talent (e.g. drawing, art and crafts), in other areas such as language (i.e. reading, spelling and writing), they experience more difficulty.

Irrespective of whether the problem is dyslexia or a child being a slow learner, it is critical that parents follow up early to get extra help for their children. By at least the 2nd Grade of schooling (age around 7 years), there ought to be signs of learning problems and at that stage, there ought to be intervention.

Early Intervention is Important

The kinds of difficulties experienced by children with dyslexia are not something that will somehow pass them by. It is **not** just "a phase they are going through" or something that they will "grow out of." It generally will not suddenly "click" one day or "click into place" for the student.

There are many parents who have sat in my office and regretted the day that they felt there was something amiss with their children and their learning ability and they felt something was wrong, but somehow or other they did not act on it. They couldn't quite put their finger on it, but they just had this intuition or this feeling. It just didn't seem right.

Once they approached the teacher, however, they were assured that everything was fine, or that it was just a phase the child was going through and that everything would be fine in the end. Perhaps they were just being a "neurotic" parent and that there was nothing really to worry about.

How do you think those parents feel five or 10 years later when they sit in my office and realize that all the while, their son or daughter had dyslexia or a specific learning problem? They feel anger. They want to go straight back to that school and abuse someone. They feel guilty. They feel remorseful. They become teary. They beat up on themselves because they did not act on their intuitions.

In hindsight, it is always very easy to see how perhaps you could have done it differently. We are always good with our hindsight vision.

The message is clear. **Act on your intuitions**. If you as a parent have this sense or this niggling feeling that something is not quite right, then step out and have your child tested by a psychologist.

**Do NOT Feel the pain of regret.
If you think your child has a learning problem, get him or her tested by an educational or school psychologist.**

Your school should be able to indicate whether the Education Department psychologist or school psychologist could undertake this task effectively within a reasonable timeline. Not all school psychologists (sometimes called Guidance Officers) are able to be in a position to complete extensive testing and sometimes the waiting list is too long. Under these circumstances, you would be better off making an appointment with a private psychologist who is subsidized by private health care.

If you find in the end that the child is fine and that there was no cause for concern, then it is still money well spent. You still have a detailed profile and report on your child's intellectual abilities. More importantly, you do not want to feel pain of regret.

Further, **early intervention is critical. The earlier the better.** Generally speaking, if there is a learning disorder, then it usually becomes obvious somewhere around the 2nd to 4th Grade of schooling.

Occasionally, of course, a really switched on kindergarten or junior primary school teacher can identify the issue in either Kindergarten or Grade 1. However, experience shows us that it is not generally until the child really starts serious reading, spelling and arithmetic at around the latter part of Grade1 or in Grade 2 and beyond that the learning issue becomes more obvious.

I remember seeing a delightful 11-year-old student in Grade 6 who was brought in to see me by her grandmother. The grandmother said that she had always suspected that her own daughter (the 11-year-old's mother) had always had dyslexia, but she had never actually had her own daughter tested.

She had noticed similar signs with her granddaughter, who did not want to read, who had a good deal of difficulty with spelling, who was slow to start and finish written

> projects and stories, who was easily distracted in class and at times disruptive.
>
> The grandmother indicated that she was wiser now and somewhat more confident in her opinion and did not want to make the same mistake with her granddaughter, who was now living with her, by not having her assessed.
>
> Her intuitions were correct. At least as far as the granddaughter goes, testing revealed she had dyslexia.

How Do You Test for Dyslexia?

The only way to test for dyslexia is to request a psychologist to do an assessment. The psychologist completes what is called a full **intellectual and educational assessment** with tests that are specifically designed for use with children and adolescents. Students enjoy the variety of tasks, some of which are familiar (e.g. spelling words) and some of which are novel (e.g. making patterns with blocks, arranging pictures).

The assessment is usually conducted using a test called "The Wechsler Intelligence Scale for Children" (i.e. WISC) which examines intelligence and highlights any cognitive strengths for the student and any weaknesses that might be creating a "learning block or barrier."

This is followed by educational assessments (e.g. various reading, spelling and arithmetic tests) to examine whether the student has fallen behind in any academic areas and if so, how far behind they might be.

How Does an Assessment help?

After the assessment, the psychologist will be able to tell you how your child compares with other children on a range of measures such as:

Frequently Asked Questions About Child Development

- intellectual ability (or intelligence) and whether your child has any particular strengths or weaknesses
- diagnose whether your child has dyslexia or is, for example, gifted in some way
- what else might be occurring that is causing concern
- academic ability and whether your child is delayed educationally in any area (e.g. reading, math) and how far behind he or she might be

The psychologist will also make **recommendations** such as:
- ideas for individual or remedial teaching programs at school
- indications of how to best help your child at home
- how to assist with emotional or behavioral problems

A comprehensive written report would then outline the results of the assessment and the various recommendations made. The report needs to be photocopied and presented to the school. Make an appointment for a week later to allow the school to become familiar with the report and then meet with them to work out an action plan that can be developed to help your child.

2. My child is not socializing with the other children at school; what should I do?

It is definitely true that as we all come in different shapes and sizes, so we come with different personality types. Some are extroverted and some are introverted. (See also question 10, "How do I help my shy child?" in the previous chapter.)

All this goes to say that some children find it easier than others to make friends. They are more outgoing and friendly and are able to interact and communicate more easily than their introverted, more reserved peers. For example, the outgoing children tend to make friends more quickly at school, they tend to have little difficulty getting into games at recess and lunch (they often lead the game or control it) and they tend not to be the last to be picked on a team. It is more of a struggle for those who are somewhat reserved and withdrawn.

Interestingly, what I have also noted is that the extroverts tend to have lots of acquaintances and friends and if they change schools, for example, they tend to collect another lot of acquaintances and friends. The introvert, on the other hand, tends to have one or two very close friends and these friendships tend to be intense and last a lifetime even though the introverts may go their own way for periods of time.

Further, it definitely takes the introvert significantly longer time to make a friend (e.g. 2 or 3 school terms at least), but when they do, they tend to be friends for life.

It is generally the introvert who has the most difficulty in socializing and making friends. In this regard, there are a number of things that parents can do:

(1) **Talk to the teacher and find out what children your child tends to associate with** both in the classroom, as well as during recess and lunch. Is there a particular child or children for example, whom your son or daughter talk to more or perhaps play with, even if on occasion, in the playground or schoolyard? If so, talk to the parent of this child and see whether there is a possibility of arranging a time when the other child might be able to come and play at your home, for say, a couple of hours on the weekend or perhaps after school. Never invite more than one child at a time. Only ever invite one child to play with your son or daughter.

(2) During the school holidays, it is also important to see if you can perhaps **arrange a special outing** such as a trip to the movies or ten pin bowling, for example, or to the local swimming pool. Again, invite one child at a time.

(3) **Talk to the teacher and see if there is any way that he or she may be able to arrange the seating in the classroom** such that your son or daughter gets to sit next to their "most preferred" or "favorite" person. Alternatively, in particular classroom activities, the

teacher may well be able to arrange for your child to interact with someone else in the class with whom they would like to be paired as a way of building up the interaction and general confidence of your child with another boy or girl in their class. Alerting the teacher to your concerns should increase the teacher's sensitivity to the issue.

(4) On occasion, parents have also offered to **take away another child during the school holidays** when they might have a trip planned to the snow, to a capital city, camping in the ranges or even on local outings. It doesn't have to be an expensive exercise.

In essence, if your child is not socializing because he generally is more reserved and shy, then it is important for parents to set up the environment for their children to assist them to interact and communicate and establish the friendships that they want.

3. What's this thing called Asperger's that I've heard about?

Asperger's Syndrome or Asperger's Disorder has up to this point largely gone unnoticed until only recently when it has been really recognized as a diagnosis affecting about 3% of children. It is generally considered to be on a continuum of autism where severe autistic-like behavior is at one end with Asperger's being at the mild end.

It appears to be more common in boys and are also appears to be a genetic characteristic in that it seems more frequent among family members of individuals who have the disorder.

The first signs of Asperger's are generally around kindergarten or preschool when motor delays or motor clumsiness might be observed. Difficulties in social interaction at school are further indicators that there might be some problems and this is followed by particular idiosyncratic interests or obsessions such as a fascination with bus timetables or twigs and branches.

The disorder generally proceeds into adulthood and as adults, individuals usually have difficulties with social communication, understanding and empathy for others.

A **diagnosis** for Asperger's would include the following:

- At least normal IQ and possibly superior IQ
- Marked problems with social interactions, not able to read social cues or non-verbals and failure to develop peer relationships
- A lack of spontaneity in sharing enjoyment, interests or achievements with others
- Difficulties with changes in routines and wanting sameness
- Being preoccupied with a specific subject of interest that is abnormal in intensity or focus (e.g. car door handles, feathers etc.)
- Overly sensitive to sounds, tastes, smells, and sights
- Have obsessive routines or rituals
- Repetitive motor movements (e.g. hand or finger flapping or twisting)

Although assessments are conducted by psychologists and psychiatrists, this is generally regarded the domain of the Autistic Association to deliver a conclusive diagnosis. Irrespective, treatment can be regarded as difficult to implement in that these children usually require dedicated educational programs in schools requiring a good deal of one-on-one attention.

4. How do I know if my child has ADD or ADHD?

The popular press used to (and still does on occasion) call it "**Hyperactivity.**" Actually, hyperactivity was the most widely studied disorder of childhood during the 1970s and 80s.

Despite recent interest in ADD, however, the general notion of hyperactivity has been around for centuries.

More recently, the labels Attention Deficit Disorder (ADD) and more particularly, Attention Deficit Hyperactivity Disorder (ADHD) have been used. It is thought that the term ADD or ADHD is more appropriate since it highlights the general agreement that the major problem in hyperactive children is paying attention, listening and concentrating.

Interestingly, I heard a colleague say recently that because so many children now seem to be diagnosed with ADD than previously, he felt that it was more a case of "Absent Discipline Disorder" than any real neurological explanation. There may well be some truth in that statement!

Definition and classification of ADHD has been a controversial question for some years. Despite decades of research, there is no single foolproof test nor consensus on what classifies ADHD. Part of the confusion comes from the fact that outwardly, ADHD children look apparently normal. Although the existence of ADHD seems to be agreed upon by clinicians and researchers, there is no uniformly acceptable definition of the disorder.

If then, the criteria are so diverse, what symptoms are available to help in the diagnosis of ADHD?

Basically, **ADHD has been defined in the following ways**:

(1) **Behavioral problems** e.g. impulsivity, over-activity, inconsistency, disorganization, clumsiness, poor self-esteem, language deficits and specific learning disabilities;

(2) An **inability to stop, look and listen** i.e. to maintain attention and concentrate;

(3) Frequent **failure to follow verbal requests or instructions**; does not seem to listen.

Possibly, the most common source of reference for diagnosis by psychologists and psychiatrists is the *"Diagnostic and Statistical Manual of Mental Disorders."* This states that the essential features of ADHD are signs of developmentally inappropriate attention, impulsivity, and hyperactivity.

How common is ADHD?

Researchers and clinicians agree that the incidence of the disorder is in the range of 1% - 5% of children.

While differences in the definitions used by professionals have an effect on the number of reported cases, it also appears that socioeconomic status (SES) influences the likelihood of the complaint as a result of poorer pre-post natal medical care and nutrition; greater likelihood of family instability; and less education and information on child development and parent management techniques. In addition, ADHD is a male-dominated complaint and as such, rates of ADHD vary between the sexes.

What causes ADHD?

The causes of ADHD are again debatable. There are widely varying opinions and arguments. Some of the factors thought to be associated with ADHD include the following:

- difficulties in central auditory processing
- cognitive weaknesses including using one's thoughts to both focus and maintain attention and effort during problem solving
- minimal brain dysfunction as evidenced by motor in-coordination and mildly abnormal reflexes
- minor physical abnormalities
- genetic factors
- dietary considerations including food additives and refined sugars
- birth complications
- chaotic home environments and psychiatric disturbance in the parents

- difficult infant temperament especially in conjunction with poor parenting

It is clear that no single factor can adequately account for the symptoms of ADHD. In fact, it is probable that there are multiple factors causing the complaint.

What are the developmental stages of the disorder?

In sequence, taking the stages of the developmental course of hyperactive children, the following patterns are often recognized:

0-2 years: 1) Not all hyperactive children show difficulties during this period, but a majority do.

2) Problems are associated with temperament including eating, fussy and irregular eaters; sleeping, disturbances in sleep patterns including shorter periods of sleep; and activity level, restlessness, difficult to hold and restrain in cribs.

2-3 years: 1) Those who were not difficult as infants now begin to show problems.

2) Problems include non-compliance, restlessness, clumsiness and being accident prone, difficulties in taking naps or playing alone without parent attention, difficulties in toilet training.

3) Parents may dismiss this period as the "terrible 2's" or transitory especially if it is the first child.

3-5 years: 1) During this phase, the parents often seek psychological help because the kindergarten or school staff also indicate that there are problems.

2) Problems include non-compliance especially in public, poor peer interactions (i.e. aggression toward other children, selfishness with own possessions, demands others possessions), destructive (i.e. due to clumsiness as well as anger), parents believe their child has less of a conscience than other children, child does not seem to be responsive to ordinary disciplinary methods, and if disciplined may become very angry, child blames others for problems, parents have difficulty finding baby-sitters and may decrease socialization with friends and other families, possibly resulting in parental depression.

5 years and older:
1) Problems at school with behavior and general performance emerge. School staff complain; decisions have to be made about keeping the child down in kindergarten because of "immaturity" or not being "school ready." Appearance of learning problems becomes highly probable, and they are not liked by other children and may become "loners" because of aggression, selfishness and clumsiness, continue to blame others for their problems, lying and petty theft may arise.

Later childhood:
1) Problems continue with failure at school (i.e. bragging, lying, cheating, truancy as a way of gaining success or acceptance) and stress at home (i.e. arguments, tensions), and the child may also show depression and low self-esteem. Acting out behavior may increase due to frustration and chronic failure, and first contact with the law for minor offences such as trespassing and verbal abuse may occur.

Does the disorder continue into adolescence and adulthood?

A number of myths exist about children outgrowing their complaints and catching up at puberty. In short, the disorder does persist into adolescence and adulthood, but not in every case. The symptoms have been found to continue into **adolescence** in about 50-80% of individuals.

In addition there are continued problems with poor academic performance, low self-image, and difficulties with peer relationships. Associated antisocial behaviors also continue into adolescence in an average of 25% of cases. Alcohol abuse and possible substance abuse, become obvious for this group.

In **adulthood**, the problems of adolescence seem to ease somewhat, partly as a result of the greater freedom given to adults. They still continue however to be impulsive, inattentive, and more restless than others. It is not yet known however, whether hyperactive children as adults are more likely to have hyperactive children than are adults with a normal background and development.

Treatment: What works?

Although ADHD cannot be cured, there are a number of treatment approaches that seem to have some success with ADHD children, such as drug management, behavior management and cognitive or "thinking" therapy.

While not all children take medication for the disorder, **drug management** is thought to help 60-70% of children who are **properly diagnosed** as hyperactive. The most common drug is Ritalin. When it is effective, behavioral improvement is almost immediate, but no-one can predict how long the medication will be needed. Drug treatment is less effective for children under 5 years of age and is generally not prescribed after the age of 16.

Drug treatment has its primary effect only on attention span, memory and impulse control (i.e. it stimulates the concentration and attending centre of the brain), and although behavioral changes occur, medication has little effect on the improvement of academic achievement. While drug treatment seems to assist in day to day management, other treatments are also required not only to assist academic performance, but also long term social adjustment and self-esteem.

Behavior management program is used in order for parents to obtain management strategies to handle their children. ADHD children seem to respond well to the structure and limits of such techniques, where the rules are explicit, and the consequences of appropriate and inappropriate behavior are given immediately.

Cognitive or "thinking" therapy focuses on children's "self-talk" as a way of teaching self-control. Children are taught strategies to stop and define the problem, consider several possible solutions before acting, monitor their own performance, and give themselves a pat on the back.

Glyco-nutritional supplements have more recently been suggested as assisting ADHD as well. There is an increasing body of research suggesting that nutritional supplements are having positive effects for children with attention and concentration difficulties.

In summary, a variety of factors working together are likely to be the causes of ADHD. Major symptoms include: poor attention and short-term memory; distractibility; impulsive and silly behavior which is sometimes dangerous to self and others; poor self-esteem and other emotional and psychological reactions. Treatment and control of the disorder is effective in the majority of cases, with the use of drug treatment combined with behavior management and cognitive therapy.

5. What should I do if my child is being picked on and bullied by other children at school?

Bullying cannot be tolerated in any environment, especially in the school setting, when the impact on self-esteem can be damaging and often lifelong.

According to the literature, bullying is actually defined as "a desire to hurt **plus** hurtful action **plus** a power imbalance **plus** (usually) repetition **plus** a sense of being oppressed on the part of the victim **plus** enjoyment or pleasure on the part of the aggressor."

Bullying, however, can take a number of forms including:
- **(1)** Physical (pushing, punching, hitting, pinching, biting)
- **(2)** Verbal (put-downs, teasing, sarcasm)
- **(3)** Emotional (exclusion from the group, rumors, gossip, hiding pens, books etc.)
- **(4)** Racial (comments about appearance, language, culture)
- **(5)** Sexual (harassment, touching, gesturing)

A special note too about a new trend in the last few years called "**Cyber-bullying**." This is the use of cell phones or mobile phones to send texts to a victim. It's particularly relevant for those older children who may own a phone. Cyber-bullying can also be played out via MSN or other chat websites on the internet. It is lethal because it is usually ongoing. In other words, you can't get away from it! It's just not restricted to school.

None of these forms can be tolerated at school or in any other context and situation. This is destructive and malicious on the part of the bully.

As an overview, research on bullying shows the following kinds of statistics and trends:
- at least 15% of students in schools are involved
- about 9% are victims
- about 7% bully others repeatedly
- more students in younger grades are victimized
- boys are more likely to be bullies than girls
- by age 24, 60% of identified bullies have a criminal conviction
- bullies lose their popularity as they get older
- bullying is one of the most under-rated and enduring problems in schools today
- schools are a prime location for bullying
- studies in Canada show that bullying occurs once every 7 minutes on average, and that bullying episodes are brief, approx 37 seconds long

- the majority of bullying occurs in or close to school buildings
- most victims are unlikely to report bullying
- the emotional scars from bullying can last a lifetime
- children who are repeatedly victimized sometimes see suicide as their only escape
- only 25% of students report that teachers intervene in bullying situations, while 71% of teachers believe that they always intervene
- many adults do not know how to intervene in bullying situations and therefore, bullying is often overlooked

Why does the bully do it and what causes it?

Let's be aware of an important life rule: people do what works for them. In other words, you act and behave in ways that at some level, you perceive work for you. You get a "payoff." So, what pay-off does the bully get? Answer: power and control.

So, what causes it? A number of different factors have been identified as contributing to bullying problems.

(1) Family Factors
- a lack of attention, warmth and love
- poor supervision of the child
- poor parenting skills
- come from homes where physical punishment is used
- modeling of aggressive behavior at home including physical and verbal aggression toward the child by the parents and/or use of physical and verbal aggression by the parents towards each other

(2) Individual Factors
- difficult temperament (moody, temper tantrums)
- active, impulsive temperament (on the go, acts as if driven by a motor)
- physical strength (with boys)
- do not take responsibility for their actions (blame the victim for provoking them)

(3) School Factors
- low levels of supervision, particularly in the playground, schoolyard and hallways and corridors.
- appropriateness of interventions by adults when they witness bullying or are made aware of it
- curricula and administrative policies that are not clearly defined on bullying

Who bullies more: girls or boys?

A researcher named Olweus reported in 1993 that a study of students in Norway in Grades 5 to 7 found that 60% of girls who were bullied were bullied only by boys, while another 15-20% were bullied by both boys and girls. The great majority of boys who were bullied (80%) were bullied only by boys. This shows that it is **boys** who are more likely to be perpetrators of "direct" bullying which involves direct physical or verbal attacks.

Olweus also concluded that **girls** are more likely to use indirect, subtle, social means to harass other girls. This includes social exclusion from groups, manipulation of friendship relationships, and spreading of rumors and gossip.

Overall, the patterns of bullying and victimization are very different for boys and girls.

Interestingly too, the **long-term outlook for bullies** is not good. The pattern of bullying often becomes **a habit** as the bully gets older.

Bullies have average social popularity up to approximately age 14 or 15 years. In fact, some children even look up to bullies in some ways because they seem to be powerful and do what they want to, to get their own way with their peers.

By late adolescence, however, the bully's popularity begins to wane. By senior secondary school, if a bully is still attending school, he or she starts to hang around with other bullies or more seriously, he or she becomes part of a gang.

By this stage, regular bullying incidents are often a thing of the past, but all victims know who the bullies are and avoid them.

By late secondary school or high school, school-yard bullying continues to be a rare occurrence, but what takes its place is often more serious. **By age 24, studies show that up to 60 percent of people who are identified as childhood bullies have at least one criminal conviction.**

Who are the victims?

Research shows that 60% of all students are never involved in any kind of bullying incidents, either as victims or as bullies. Nevertheless, for that small percentage (9%) who are victims, they are characterized by the following:
- typically anxious, insecure and cautious
- often quiet or shy
- low self-esteem
- rarely defend themselves or retaliate when confronted by students who bully them and are therefore "safe" targets for the bully
- often lack social skills and friends and may be socially isolated
- may have parents who could be described as overprotective
- tend to be physically weaker than their peers
- stand out in a different way (e.g. color of their hair, manner of speech)
- stand out in some positive way (e.g. very good at math or science)

Many children will not let on that they are being bullied at school. Typically, they may not let on because they are deeply afraid of the following:

(1) they are afraid of any further payback if the bully finds out
(2) they don't want the parents to go to the school and somehow embarrass them or make a fuss
(3) they don't want the teachers to know that they can't handle it
(4) they don't want to look or sound weak or 'pathetic'

(5) they don't want to be seen as someone getting others into trouble

In our experience, that is the order of factors by which children report to us that they do not want to report on the bully.

Although your child may **not** tell you initially that he or she is being bullied, typically, the **top three tell-tale signs** include the following:
- continual stomach "upsets" or headaches that means that they need to stay home, or frequent visits to the school sick room, or being sent home because they are unwell
- obvious panic or anxiety about going to school
- trouble sleeping at night and awakening often through the night, or difficulty dropping off to sleep

Other signs include things such as:
- wanting the parent to drop them off at the school gate rather than take the bus or walk or ride a bike
- becoming short-tempered, intolerant, with perhaps some outbursts
- becoming teary, withdrawn or depressed
- a drop-off in grades or in the standard of their schoolwork
- a hint of school refusal
- saying that they want to kill themselves
- not eating or eating excessively
- crying themselves to sleep and having nightmares
- asking for extra pocket money or maybe stealing (in order to keep the bully happy)
- unexplained bruises, cuts, scratches and / or damaged clothing
- have their possessions go missing
- refusing to say what's wrong

Sadly, we have often heard well-meaning parents say the following kinds of things to their own children or about other children who could be considered bullies:
- "I was bullied at school and it didn't do me any harm"

Frequently Asked Questions About Child Development

- "You'll just have to learn to stand up for yourself"
- "Tell him to hit back, only harder"
- "It's character building"
- "Sticks and stones may break your bones, but names can never hurt you"
- "That's not bullying! It's just kids teasing"

Wrong. Well-meaning maybe, but wrong. None of these statements are true.

> **Telling your child to just "ignore the bully" doesn't work. It's a glib throw away line that might be well-intentioned, but useless.**

The other well-meaning piece of advice that parents often give to their children is "ignore it." Save your breath. Ignoring doesn't work. It never did and it never will. You need something more significant and substantial in order to handle a bully.

What to do about the bullying?

Clearly, the bullying has to stop. The impact on self-esteem can be very severe and damaging – at times, permanent. Try following these steps:

- ✓ **Listen – really listen.** Just hold your tongue and quietly repeat back what you have heard as well as quietly ask questions to make sure that you fully understand what has gone on.

- ✓ **Don't judge & keep calm** – be supportive and understanding. Don't start to get agitated and declare what you'd like to do to the bully or put the school down or anything else. This is a time for steadiness and care.

- ✓ **Ask, don't tell** – ask your children, "What do you think should happen now?" Remember that this is their torment and anguish and they have to live in this situation daily. So don't begin to trot out remedies and solutions until, at the very least, you have asked your child what she thinks should occur.

- ✓ Perhaps **prompt with questions** like: "Is there any way, I wonder, that you could get him / her to stop bullying you?" or "What might happen if you pretended you didn't hear them?" or "What would they do if you just walked away?"

- ✓ If your child says **"Don't tell the teacher"** – Ask gently why not – What is his fear? Quietly talk it through. Don't push. Your child is already terrified of the bully, you as the parent don't need to increase his fear levels by threatening to march on down to the school to "sort it all out."

- ✓ **If it's OK to talk to the teacher, do so discretely** – perhaps find out before how the teacher might handle it first. Not all teachers have had experience in handling bullying. Therefore, find a teacher who has had experience in dealing with bullying, not a teacher who might be well-meaning. We have had some very well-meaning teachers and principals who have made a fiasco of it all and have done such outrageous things as introduced the victim to the bully and attempted to get them to "be friends" or "resolve their differences and conflict." Disastrous. This has only served to increase the bully's power as he or she knows that the victim is worried, anxious, scared and the victim in turn, is now terrified! Literally so. **Definitely, there should be no exposure of the victim.**

- ✓ If you are **not happy with the teacher's response** – be prepared to talk to the principal about it. The bully needs to be brought in for a serious discussion and the parents or family involved. If the bullying continues, then the bully ought to be removed from the school. If you are not happy with the school's response, you may need to consider leaving altogether

- ✓ **Check how your child is going** – don't nag or always be asking – and watch for any tell-tale signs of continuing distress (e.g. stomach aches, not wanting to go to school etc.)

It is to be hoped that the school has a strong anti-harassment policy, which includes bullying, that is just not words on paper and it is hoped that the staff have all had workshops on the topic and know clearly what to do and when. Students should also be aware of and have been made familiar with the policy.

In fact, if you haven't already, then seek an appointment with your school principal and ask not only what your school's discipline policy might be, but more specifically, what your school's policy on bullying is and **what procedurally and operationally do they actually do** when a case of bullying is brought to their attention. Expect to be given not just a platitude of nice-sounding words, but actual procedural steps about what the school would do when a case of bullying is identified. Anything less is either negligence or ignorance on the school's behalf.

If help is not forthcoming from your school, it may be worthwhile enlisting the help of the overall governing body responsible for the school (e.g. the District Education Office, the Catholic Education Office, the Association of Independent

Schools etc.) who could work with the school staff to address the problem. If all else fails, then your child who is being victimized needs to leave and find another school to attend.

6. My child doesn't want to go to school and I'm having terrible trouble getting him there each day.

In my clinical experience, this kind of situation generally arises because of both the nature of the child being somewhat anxious and timid in the first place, along with other external situations such as bullying or a problem with the teacher.

Certainly, it is also true to say that any of these factors alone, such as having a somewhat fearful child or the child being exposed to particular external factors, could create a situation of school refusal.

Note that if refusal to go to school is the only area of non-compliance, i.e. the child is generally cooperative in every other area, then the reason behind the reluctance needs to be immediately explored.

Of course, such situations if they do arise are relatively traumatic for everyone concerned. The whole family tends to get involved when parents feel tense and perhaps helpless, the child feels distraught and the teachers sometimes are not able to suggest strategies that might assist.

What typically happens in these kinds of scenarios is that the night before school, the child starts to complain about not wanting to go to school next day. The child may also have difficulty getting off to sleep and may come out of their bedroom a number of times perhaps complaining about a stomach-ache or a headache.

The next morning, the child could be loath to get out of bed and start to protest about going to school. Often they start to feel sick and do not want to eat breakfast. Typically, they will not want to get dressed and if the arguments between the parent and the child haven't started up until this point, then this is usually the time when the parent starts to feel particularly helpless, and often begins to become angry. Needless to say, the child becomes teary.

The trip in the car to school is often consumed by the child becoming very teary and the parent trying to reassure and cajole. At the time of separating in the schoolyard or in the classroom, when the parent says goodbye is often the time of heightened tears and in many cases hysteria on the part of the child.

Not surprisingly, the parent (and it is usually the mother) starts to become distraught seeing their child in so much anguish and pain.

In many cases, the child could well be characterized by being anxious overall. More often than not, this is a family characteristic where the mother for example, may also describe herself as a "worrier" or a "worry wart."

Typically, the kinds of scenarios that might occur in this situation could include the following:
- the parent is overprotective, constantly checking with the child to see if he or she is okay and generally triggering the child's anxiety
- the child believes that the mother in particular might die and consequently, the child is loath to leave the mother's side
- the child believes that the mother is sufficiently "neurotic" or anxious herself that the child is worried about the mother's welfare and feels the need to stay home to look after the parent

> Andrew was a somewhat timid but delightful 7-year-old who presented with his mother Sue because the situation at home and at school had reached crisis point.

> His mother reported that Andrew was particularly frightened about going to school, and it had now eventuated that he was crying and screaming at the point of separation in the classroom or outside the classroom, and to the extent where he was almost dry-reaching or dry-heaving.
>
> Through discussion, it evolved that two weeks previously, Andrew had forgotten to take his hat to school which meant that under the school policy, he was not allowed to play in the playground or on the oval in the sun at recess or lunch. He had become particularly tearful and upset and felt somewhat mortified that he had "gotten into trouble."
>
> The next day, his mother began to become overprotective, rechecking that he had not forgotten anything before they left for school, and she also began to ask Andrew frequently in the car on the way to school if he was okay. Needless to say, this only heightened Andrew's anxiety, to the point where the situation deteriorated and professional help was required.
>
> As an aside, intervention required that the mother put aside her own fears and that she stop asking Andrew questions about how he was feeling. As for Andrew, it was decided that since he had a vivid imagination, he would create a superhero in his mind to be with him at school, and to give him the strength he desired.
>
> It certainly worked. Andrew was delighted with his new found internal strength, and his mother was greatly relieved.

Irrespective, it is generally true to say that **there is always a trigger that precipitates these school refusals**.

Typically, the kinds of things that might have occurred for the child could include the following:

- the child believes that he or she has no friends at school and no one to play with and feels particularly isolated, especially at recess and lunchtimes
- bullying by some other student or students from their own class or from others in the school; such bullying could occur in the classroom, or more likely occurs in the playground
- the child has a learning disorder, or dyslexia, that has not been identified and as such, the child is struggling at school, starting to fall behind and perhaps failing in some areas
- the child is conscious of a major event approaching such as a school camp where they are becoming fearful about being away from home particularly if they're not feeling supported in the school setting
- the teacher or the teacher's style is particularly negative, where he or she tends to be highly critical, pick on or target particular students, embarrass students publicly, and raise his or her voice unnecessarily

So the motto overall is to ensure firstly that you as the parent "do not project your own fears onto your child." Be aware of what you say and how you say it, and if you're feeling anxious or worried yourself be very careful that you do not transmit this to your child. Children generally have excellent radar and can pick up the vibes of the parent, so as a parent, it is your job to make sure that what you transmit is positive and reassuring.

Secondly, have a talk to your child, perhaps at night as you are putting her to bed or give her a special cuddle when she gets home from school and ask about what is going well at school and what is not going particularly well.

Ask for example, about how she is doing at reading, spelling, mathematics and writing. Ask about how she might be getting along with the other students and who her best friends might be. Ask how much she likes her teacher and what it is that she both likes and dislikes about her teacher. Listen very carefully to what she says.

If you find that the issue might be in relation to say, lack of friends and feeling alone especially at play time, then see the comments above under question 2. If you discover that the problem about not wanting to go to school is due to some bullying, then see the comments under question 5 above. If you believed that your child might be struggling academically, then see the comments under question 1 above. If it is really the parent's own anxiety and fears, then being able to discuss it with a professional such as a psychologist could assist.

The answer to your child's refusal to go to school is likely to be either a feature of his or her own anxious personality and/or a feature of some trigger that has set it all off.

"It is a miracle that curiosity survives formal education."

(Albert Einstein; 1879-1955 German-born physicist)

"The illiterate of the 21st century will not be those who cannot read and write, but those who cannot learn, unlearn and re-learn."

(Alvin Toffler; American writer & futurist)

CHAPTER 8 SUMMARY

1. How do I know if my child has a Specific Learning Disorder or "Dyslexia"?

What is a Specific Learning Disorder or Dyslexia?
It is generally believed that specific learning disorders are due to a neurological or cognitive weakness; in other words, a small part of the brain is not processing information appropriately.

How Common is It?
Roughly 10% of students have a learning problem such as dyslexia. We are not therefore talking about a rare or unusual problem.

How Do You Recognize Dyslexia?
There are several common characteristics of learning problems, but is it unlikely that a student would show all of them.

Why Does it Occur?
Clinically speaking, there are primarily **three main reasons** why it occurs:
1. Heredity
2. Problems in the pregnancy
3. Problems at birth

Can it be Cured?
Because it is basically a brain processing problem, it has been present essentially from birth and so, along with the rest of our features (e.g. eye color, skin color etc.), what we have got, we have got! But, as with most of us, we learn to work around our so-called difficulties.

Early Intervention is Important
The earlier the better. Generally speaking, if there is a learning disorder, then it usually becomes obvious somewhere around Year 1 to 3.

How Do You Test for Dyslexia?
The only way to test for dyslexia is to request a psychologist to do an assessment. The psychologist completes what is called a full *intellectual and educational assessment* with tests that are specifically designed for use with children and adolescents.

How Does an Assessment help?
The psychologist will be able to tell you if your child has any learning problems, whether your son / daughter is behind in their development (and if so, how far), if he or she has "dyslexia" and will also make recommendations about what you and the school can do.

2. My child is not socializing with the other children at school; what should I do?
It is important for parents to set up the environment for their children to assist them to interact and communicate and establish the friendships that they want. Four tips are provided as a way of assisting in this regard.

3. What's this thing called Asperger's that I've heard about?
It is generally considered to be on a continuum of autism where severe autistic-like behavior is at one end with Asperger's being at the mild end. It only occurs in about 3% of children, is more common amongst boys and the signs of Asperger's usually start to show at around pre-school or the first year or two of school.

4. How do you know if your child has ADD or ADHD?

The popular press used to (and still does on occasion) call it "**Hyperactivity.**" Around 1 - 5% of children have this disorder. The essential features of ADHD are signs of developmentally inappropriate attention, impulsivity, and hyperactivity.

It is caused by a number of factors, but it is essentially a "brain" problem that is there from birth where information to the brain is not processed properly. Symptoms have been found to continue into adolescence in about 50-80% of individuals.

Treatment has been multi-modal in that strict behavioral programs are important to have in place, along with drug therapy in some instances, although there is some evidence of glyco-nutritional supplements being helpful.

5. What should I do if my child is being picked on and bullied by other children at school?

Bullying cannot be tolerated in any environment, especially in the school setting when the impact on self-esteem can be damaging and often lifelong.

The issue must be raised at school and to this end, the parent has to find a compassionate, caring teacher who knows what to do. Under no circumstances should there be exposure of the victim.

6. My child doesn't want to go to school and I'm having terrible trouble getting him there each day.

This kind of situation generally arises because the child being somewhat anxious and timid in relation to temperament, along with other external situations such as bullying, a learning difficulty or a problem with the teacher.

Certainly, the answer to your child's refusal to go to school will likely be either as a feature of his own anxious personality and / or as a feature of some trigger that has set it all off.

CHAPTER 9

EPILOGUE

Finally, parenting along with being a marriage partner or permanent partner is one of the most difficult roles that I know. Both roles come with **no** real training or instruction. We tend to "fly by the seat of our pants."

Somehow or other, we get it more or less right. Naturally, in hindsight we can often see where we could have done it differently, but then of course, that's the distinct advantage of hindsight. Nevertheless, we gave it our best shot. Our children could ask for nothing more.

Of course, we didn't get it perfect and, of course, there are numerous things that maybe we would have done differently given another chance. Irrespective, we were well-intended and we wanted to do it "right".

A final story. A story about eagles; those majestic birds. It is not my story; it's from David McNally, (*"Even Eagles Need a Push"*, 1990), but one that is relevant here. He states as follows:

The eagle gently coaxed her offspring toward the edge of the nest. Her heart quivered with conflicting emotions as she felt their resistance to her persistent nudging. "Why does the thrill of soaring have to begin with the fear of falling?" she thought. This ageless question was still unanswered for her.

As in the tradition of the species, her nest was located high on the shelf of a sheer rock face. Below there was nothing but air to support the wings of each child. "Is it possible that this time it will not work?" she thought. Despite her fears, the eagle knew it was time. Her parental mission was all but complete. There remained one final task – the push.

The eagle drew courage from an innate wisdom. Until her children discovered their wings, there was no purpose for their lives. Until they learned how to soar, they would fail to understand the privilege it was to have been born an eagle. The push was the greatest gift that she had to offer. It was her supreme act of love. And so one by one, she pushed them, and they flew!

That is the parental role in giving our children the confidence to finally fly and the confidence to soar.

We do it by the delicate balance of love and rules. It is my sincere desire that you will feel empowered and strengthened from taking the practical applications from this book.

Blessings in your parenting.

ABOUT THE AUTHOR

Dr Darryl Cross is both a clinical and organizational psychologist as well as a life coach together with being an international speaker, author and university lecturer.

As a **psychologist**, he is a Fellow of the Australian Psychological Society as well as an Affiliate of the American Psychological Association. He is also a Fellow of the Australian Institute of Management.

He gained his initial degree in Psychology from Flinders University of South Australia before completing his doctorate in Psychology at the University of Queensland in Australia.

Dr Cross **lectured** in post-graduate psychology at both the University of Queensland and at Macquarie University in Sydney, New South Wales including courses in clinical psychology, counseling and school counseling. He currently is a sessional lecturer in various post-graduate (Masters & Doctorate) courses at the University of South Australia.

While in Queensland, he acted as a consultant to the Catholic Family Welfare Agency and had a part-time private practice. Following a return to Adelaide in South Australia, Darryl became the director of a unit for children with severe behavioral disorders at the Adelaide Women's & Children's Hospital which he held for three years before beginning his own private practice which he has been in for the last 19 years.

As a **personal coach**, Dr Cross initially completed the Professional Development Certificate in Coaching Practice through the Department of Psychology at the University of Sydney, and in 2006, completed graduate studies in coaching in California, USA. He is now a Certified Personal & Executive Coach, from the College of Executive Coaching and is a Professional Certified Coach with the International Coach Federation.

As a **speaker**, Dr Cross is a member of the National Speakers Association and has conducted countless workshops on numerous topics including parenting, adolescents, increasing self-confidence, dealing with conflict, and the art of listening. He has also given scores of key-note addresses to various conferences and gatherings in various countries such as Malaysia, the United Kingdom, and the USA.

As an **author**, he has published numerous academic papers for national and overseas journals, as well as articles for the popular press and written the book, *"Teenager Trouble-Shooting."*

He has also authored manuals on *"How to Stop Your Self-Sabotage: Steps to Increase Your Self-Confidence"* and *"Listen Up Now! How to increase profit and growth in business by really listening to your clients & customers."*

Academic study as well as life experience, and being a psychologist as well as coach for over 30 years means that Dr Cross has come up with practical ways to use principles of life that work.

He understands human behavior and therefore can help individuals and teams to move to another place. He has the knack of being able to say it all simply.

Address: Crossways Consulting
PO Box 2000,
North Adelaide
South Australia
AUSTRALIA   5006

www.drdarryl.com
www.growingupchildren.com
www.teenagertroubleshooting.com

Made in the USA
San Bernardino, CA
02 April 2018